Margaret Thatcher-
First Lady of the House

Margaret Thatcher-
First Lady of the House

Ernle Money

Leslie Frewin of London

First published 1975 by
Leslie Frewin Publishers Limited,
Five Goodwin's Court,
Saint Martin's Lane,
London WC2N 4LL, England

Printed in Great Britain by Page Bros (Norwich) Ltd

Bound by Dorstel Press, Harlow

ISBN 0 85632 193 1

FOR SUE

'Neque enim sexum in imperiis discernunt. . .'

They (the British) recognise no distinction between the sexes in choosing their leaders . . .

Tacitus *Agricola* 16

Contents

Acknowledgements

I should like to express my gratitude to all who have helped me in the preparation of this book, both to those who are mentioned in the text and to many other people who have given generously of their time and help. In particular I am very grateful to Harold Soref, without whom the book would not have come into existence in the first place, Percy Ramchandani, Derek Howe, Norman Neill-Fraser, Stewart Dewar and to Fiona Cierach who typed the manuscript with such patience and skill. I am also indebted to the editors and staff of the *East Anglian Daily Times* and *Grantham Journal*, to the librarians and staff of the Grantham, Westminster and Woodbridge public libraries, and to all the staff of my publishers for their assistance. Finally, I am grateful to my own family for putting up with the trials of having a writer as well as a politician about the house.

Rendlesham, Suffolk, 1975   EM

Illustrations

With Princess Margaret at a Buckingham Palace Garden Party for exchange teachers in 1972 (*Press Association*)

Mrs Thatcher in her new office, which she designed herself, when the Education Department moved to Elizabeth House near Waterloo Station (*Keystone Press Agency*)

The Minister of Education, Mrs Margaret Thatcher, with (*left*) Norman St John Stevas, welcome Lord Sandford, the new Parliamentary Under-Secretary of Education, on his arrival to take up his new post (*Central Press*)

Margaret Thatcher with William Whitelaw during the leadership election contest, 1975 (*Camera Press*)

Mrs Thatcher jubilant after hearing the result of the first ballot for the leadership (*Camera Press*)

The new Tory leader at her first Press Conference (*Central Press*)

Margaret Thatcher outside her Chelsea home after her victory in the Conservative Party leadership election (*Keystone Press Agency*)

Mr and Mrs Denis Thatcher, 1975 (*Camera Press*)

With Michael Heseltine at a rally at Central Hall, Westminster, February 1975 (*Keystone Press Agency*)

Margaret Thatcher with Pierre Trudeau, Prime Minister of Canada (*Keystone Press Agency*)

Mrs Thatcher with the US Secretary of State, Henry Kissinger (*Keystone Press Agency*)

Madame Françoise Giroud, the French Minister for Women, and Margaret Thatcher, find something to amuse them at the opening of the Women and Power Conference in London in April 1975 (*Keystone Press Agency*)

Margaret Thatcher with Ronald Reagan, American ex-actor and ex-Senator (*Press Association*)

Mrs Thatcher at the Conservative Women's Conference, May 1975 (*Keystone Press Agency*)

Mrs Thatcher has tea with the staff of the new Paris branch of Marks and Spencer, May 1975 (*Keystone Press Agency*)

Margaret Thatcher meets the French President, Valery Giscard D'Estaing (*Keystone Press Agency*)

With William Whitelaw at a meeting to boost the Tory campaign to keep Britain in the Common Market (*Central Press*)

At the European Parliament with Peter Kirk (*right*) (*Conservative Central Office*)

Margaret Thatcher at the door of the show house at the Ideal Homes Exhibition, Olympia, March 1975 (*Keystone Press Agency*)

In Edinburgh during her tour of Scotland (*Camera Press*)

Mrs Margaret Thatcher, after registering her vote in the Common Market Referendum, June 1975 (*Central Press*)

1

Background to Conflict

Throughout 11th October, 1974, it became increasingly obvious that the Conservative Party had been defeated at a general election for the second time during the course of that year. Although the Socialists had won by only a narrow overall margin, taking less than 40% of the total number of votes polled, they had gained a bare absolute majority in the House of Commons, which was probably likely to prove stronger than it looked because of the number of Liberal and nationalist members also elected. Whereas in February, when although Labour had gained the largest number of seats they had had less votes than the Conservatives, the Tory share of the poll was now down to a record low.

By the time that a grim-faced Edward Heath had conceded defeat it was already evident that his continued leadership of the party was going to come under fire from a number of quarters. He had long had his opponents within the party, some dating back as early as the 1960s when, as President of the Board of Trade, he had upset thousands of small shopkeepers over the abolition of Resale Price Maintenance, and others of more recent date since the controversies over the sacking of Enoch Powell from the Shadow Cabinet and, subsequently, over entry into Europe. Somewhat unfairly, he had also been made the scapegoat for the country's economic difficulties following a world financial crisis, so that during the period of his government there were a number in the Conservative ranks who had become increasingly disenchanted with his policies. Among these, within hours of the result, several were quick to voice their criticisms. Nicholas Winterton, the MP for Macclesfield, for instance, who had been an outspoken critic of the leader since he had come into the House at a by-election in 1972, now stated publicly that the party must look for a more sensible, grass-roots politician. 'While I have a great respect for Mr Heath's integrity and honesty.' he said, 'his style of leadership does not appeal to the mass of the electors.' The following morning, *The Times* printed a cartoon of Labour supporters looking at a pile of 'Down with Heath' placards. 'Perhaps,' one of them is saying, 'we could sell them to the Tories.'

In a number of ways the October election of 1974 could be considered less as an event on its own and more as a replay of its predecessor in February. If the nation's verdict then had been generally unexpected, it had also been largely indecisive. A Conservative Government, with at least twelve months of its original mandate to run, had decided to go to the country on the issue of whether it wanted to be governed by Parliament or the unions. The possibility of such an election had been in the air for some time. What eventually precipitated it was the state of emergency caused by a combination of the oil crisis following on the Middle East war and the fuel shortage caused by a work-to-rule on the part of the miners in support of their further wage demands. The possibility of a major breakdown in fuel resources, following this confrontation, had put the economy on a three-day week. There was little doubt that the government's previous reversal over a power strike in 1972 had already seriously damaged their position in the eyes of the public.

This time the issue which they wanted to put before the electors was a vital one—the sovereignty of Parliament itself; but, in the event, they were side-tracked into holding an election which was fought mainly on food prices. Although many people were seriously disquieted by what had been going on in the light of recent events, a fair number had come to doubt the capacity of a Conservative government to cope with a continuing confrontation with militant leaders in the unions or to win if it came to a showdown. There was a tendency, even in industry itself, to argue that the country must be got back to work as quickly as possible, whatever the cost. Edward Heath and his principal advisers waited too long before deciding to hold an election, if they were going to do so.

Talks dragged on between ministers and the TUC leaders at Downing Street until 15th January, 1974, when they reached a deadlock. The General Secretary of the TUC, Len Murray, insisted that the government should treat the miners' wage claim as a special case and come to an agreement that it should be settled outside the terms of Phase Three of the prices and incomes policy that had been approved by Parliament. If they did, he indicated that the other unions would be willing not to use any such settlement as a lever in pressing their own demands, though there was no formal way of binding them, outside the terms of Phase Three. The implications of such a settlement against the background of an already deteriorating world economic climate and rapidly increasing inflation in

Britain, were obvious. William Whitelaw, who had recently returned from a successful period as Secretary of State for Northern Ireland, to take up the equally hot-seat job of Employment, indicated that this would destroy the whole basis of the government's strategy against inflation. Although he had gained a reputation as a conciliator in his previous job, there was obviously a limit beyond which he and his colleagues felt they could not be pushed. Nevertheless, he said that they were willing to continue to negotiate for any agreement within the existing legal framework.

The press, increasingly, began to talk of a general election as the only way to secure a government with a strong enough backing to deal with the crisis. Many papers pointed to the urgency of this in the light of increasingly threatening world economic conditions. On Friday, 18th January, however, the Prime Minister, apparently taking heart from the decision of the Saudi Arabian Government to release more oil for Britain, with the consequent hope that an improved fuel situation could bring industry back to at least a four-day week, announced his intention of having another attempt to look for a solution with the TUC under Phase Three. As he was later rightly to claim, no Prime Minister of recent times had in fact spent so much time in talking with the unions but in doing so, though he proved the honesty of his intentions, he was allowing time to slip away.

On the following Thursday, the executive of the National Union of Mineworkers announced that they proposed to hold a pit-head ballot to decide whether their members wanted to extend their existing restrictions on full work into a full strike. If this became effective, production in the coalfields could be brought to a complete halt within a matter of days.

Ominously for the Conservatives, on the same day an opinion poll by the Opinion Research Centre, which had been showing a Tory lead of 5% in December and 4% in early January, now showed the Socialists to have gone into the lead by 3%. However justified ministers might have been in continuing to try to find a settlement, they were starting to get the blame for handling the crisis badly.

On Monday 28th January, Lord Carrington, the Minister for Power, warned that, faced with a major threat to cut coal supplies, there might be a need to reduce steel production by as much as two-thirds and Britain could find herself on a two-day week. Pressure on Edward Heath for an election was mounting; only now, rather than acting from a position of strength, he seemed to have little alternative. On 31st January he made one more effort to persuade the unions to accept talks on the basis of Phase Three, on the lines that if the pits went back to full-time production, the Pay Board's Relativities Report could be used to provide increases for the miners while their long-term demands could be the subject of continued talks.

The miners themselves, in the meantime, had been voting throughout the previous day on the question of a full-scale strike. The results, when they became known the following Saturday, showed that there was an overwhelming majority in favour of strike action. 'The miners have made it quite clear,' stated Len Murray, 'that this means cash on the table and, if that is their definition of acceptability, then it is the definition which we say has got to be accepted by everyone concerned.' The alternative would be a nationwide mine-workers strike from midnight on Sunday, 10th February. At the same time that Len Murray's statement was issued, the meeting between Senior Ministers and the TUC representatives at 10 Downing Street, called to try and find a solution in terms of the Relativities Report, broke down.

On Thursday morning the full cabinet met to consider the position. That same afternoon Edward Heath came to speak to a crowded meeting of Conservative backbenchers of the 1922 Committee. He announced that an election would be called for 28th February. The time given for holding it was one of the shortest in living memory and, although eventually the question of a strike was deferred pending the outcome of the election, neither side had really recovered from the restrictions of a three-day week to be in a position to be fully ready for a campaign.

The outcome was that an election which had been called by the Conservatives on the issue of moderation against extremism became directed into other topics. It was the effects of inflation rather than their cause which became the principal ground, and disillusioned reporters began to find that an election which had opened at so urgent a level was rapidly deteriorating into a series of arguments at local level over the price of fish fingers.

When the results came through on television during the night of 28th February/1st March, neither side could really be said to have won. The Conservatives, who had been leading during the last week in five of the six national opinion polls, had certainly suffered a major setback. Labour eventually gained a total of 301 seats against the Tories' 296, as compared with their previous ratio of 287 to 323. The Conservatives, however, had actually received 38·1% of the votes as opposed to Labour's 37·2%. To the dismay of both the major parties, the Liberals, who were subsequently to suffer a decline in October, increased both their share of the vote and, as many people felt, unfairly, to a far lesser degree their share in the number of seats. In Scotland, Wales and Northern Ireland, the Scottish National Party, Plaid Cymru and a United Ulster Loyalist Coalition between them gained enough members to hold the effective if disjointed balance of power in the House of Commons. One notable absentee from the new Parliament was Enoch Powell, who had announced that he would not fight again in his constituency at Wolverhampton South-West as a Conservative, and had subsequently counselled his supporters to vote Socialist, and voted Socialist himself, in the election.

There followed a period of apparently total muddle. Edward Heath approached the Liberals and the other non-Socialist parties in an attempt to reach an understanding. When this failed, the Queen sent for Harold Wilson to form a minority government. Although this had the effect of breaking the immediate deadlock, it was obvious that the electors would be subjected to a further campaign within a fairly short space of time.

It was also fairly obvious that, except for an unexpected disaster, Labour would win this when it came. As in 1966, when he had managed to turn a knife-edged majority into a comfortable working margin, Harold Wilson used his considerable political skills towards consolidating his position. Starting with the advantage of being able to rely on an initial honeymoon period with the unions, he was able to put an end to the three-day week. Except for the alarming level at which the rate of inflation was now running, everything in the country appeared to return to normality. A Socialist Government was therefore in the position of being able to call another election at the most propitious moment. Labour was then put before the voters as the party with the special advantage of getting Britain back to work. In the short session between March and July 1974, the state of the parties meant that the Opposition were largely hamstrung from pre-cipitating a crisis by defeating the government on a major issue, by the risk of creating additional public sympathy for the government as a minority admini-stration which had been turned out of office during a constitutional crisis in an irresponsible manner. A largely uneventful summer did something to allay the country's fears on inflation, and Conservative warnings as to the rate at which this was increasing were dismissed by the Chancellor of the Exchequer, Denis Healey, as grossly exaggerated. A largely uneventful election campaign in October, in which Anthony Wedgwood Benn featured nationally to a surprisingly small degree, did much to allay possible alarm as to the implications of a Socialist Government with a working majority pursuing a left-wing Socialist policy. When this election was announced in September, the government's slogan was 'Let's Win with Labour' and Harold Wilson looked to a majority of the electors to give his party the chance to put their promises into effect.

The Conservatives were left with the role of underlining the seriousness of the crisis and calling for a combination of moderate interests to oppose the effects of a swing to the left. In the run-up to the campaign one of their few effective television broadcasts which had any bite about it was from a candidates' conference at which both Willie Whitelaw and Margaret Thatcher, the shadow

Minister for Housing, spoke with considerable effect. When the time came, however, both of these were left with trying to persuade a suspicious public that a Conservative Government would mean fixed mortgage interest and rating reform, while Labour reiterated that a return to the Conservatives would entail a return to confrontation policies, while a vote for them would be a safe vote since, in the interests of consensus politics, they would avoid the more extreme measures.

In terms of their personal appearances on television, Harold Wilson also managed to get the edge on Edward Heath at this election. Although, like Nicholas Winterton, many voters admired Heath's honesty and integrity, others sensed a lack of flexibility about the Conservative leader which Wilson was quick to exploit. Sadly, many viewers did not come to accept him as a credible television figure until after his more relaxed appearances when he had finally given up the leadership, and this was to play its part. Wilson, on the other hand, was extremely effective in his performances at this time, in particular by comparison with some of his later appearances. He managed to suggest a personality which was in turns avuncular and incisive, alternating homely idiom and abrasive approach. Although at his press conferences Heath was the more impressive in terms of argument, the projection of the two leaders on television worked very much in this campaign to his opponent's advantage.

As a triumphant Harold Wilson returned to his office at Downing Street, Edward Heath was left to face the cruel realities of defeat. Despite the remarkable achievement of his victory in 1970, he was now labelled as a three-time election loser, if one included the defeat of 1966, within a year of his succeeding to Sir Alec Douglas-Home. Only a few hours after the October result the press was already rife with rumours that influential sections of the Tory party would insist that he stand down. In the Parliamentary party a crucial role would obviously lie with the Executive of the 1922 Committee, which, in Opposition, represented the main body of Conservative backbenchers as a whole. Like their leader, the Conservatives in general were licking their wounds. One difficulty was that the executive of the '22, which could normally speak for a majority of members, had been elected during the life of the last parliament and it was doubtful, strictly speaking, what validity they had to speak for the new body of members until further elections within the committee had taken place.

Another complication lay in the position of the current chairman of the Committee, Edward du Cann, the member for Taunton. Du Cann, who was acknowledged to be one of the ablest speakers in the House, had built up a considerable reputation in the City for financial expertise and had held a number of offices including Economic Secretary to the Treasury and Minister of State at the Board of Trade under Harold Macmillan and Sir Alec Douglas-Home. In 1967, however, when he was Chairman of the Conservative Party organisation, he had apparently fallen out with Edward Heath and had been preremptorily sacked from this job by him. He had not held office under the Heath Government, which made him one of the few leader figures in the party who was in no way involved with the events leading up to the disasters of 1974. He was obviously one of the main potential challengers to Heath's leadership now, if he decided to stand, but he was also the current holder of the key opposition position as Chairman of the 1922 which both added to his prestige but to some extent limited his freedom of movement.

Other names were also suggested by the press and the media. The principal ones were William Whitelaw, James Prior, Sir Christopher Soames and Sir Keith Joseph. Willie Whitelaw was one of the few members of the Heath cabinet who had become a well-known national figure and his was a name which sprang immediately to mind. The Member of Parliament for Penrith and the Border since 1955, he was a reassuring figure, large, genial and generally popular. After an outstanding war record he had come into the House with a strong feeling for public service. Although he represented an almost archetypical and so possibly slightly old-fashioned Conservative background (Winchester, Trinity College, Cambridge and a regular commission in the Scots Guards), he was personally identified with the policies of conciliation in Northern Ireland. Much of his earlier Parliamentary service had been spent in the Whips Office and he had graduated to Chief Whip and Leader of the House. He was known to be a good House of Commons man and popular with the other side, perhaps a little too popular for the likes of some of his colleagues. There were some who felt that he was too amiable a personality for the top job, in conflict with Harold Wilson, and others who resented the apparent ease with which he had identified with the party's about-turns and abandonment of the Selsdon image after 1970. He was also known to be extremely loyal to his leader and had once given great offence to the Icelandic Government by putting this into words and saying that such was his admiration for Edward Heath that he would go wherever he sent him 'even as Ambassador to Reykjavik'.

If Whitelaw was closely identified with Heath, so was James Prior. The member for Lowestoft, he had entered Parliament in 1959 and had become the leader's PPS in 1965. When he later took office in 1970 he had been appointed straight to the Cabinet as Minister of Agriculture. Like Whitelaw he was a man of considerable personal charm and integrity and was identified with moderate policies. But there was not much to choose between the two men, in the public mind, in political terms, except that Prior was some years the younger in terms of

B

age and political experience. Although, like Whitelaw, he was himself a farmer (he had a first-class degree in agriculture at Cambridge) he also had considerable experience of industry and represented a constituency which was more than a little industrial in its make-up.

It was evident that neither of those two would be prepared to start a palace revolution on their own account, whatever their particular qualifications. The possible significance of such figures among the 'Heath men' could only be if the leader decided voluntarily to withdraw and then, if they both stood, there was a real risk that their votes would cancel each other out. Another possible contender from the establishment ranks of the party did not seem to have any immediate power base at all. Sir Christopher Soames, the son-in-law of Winston Churchill, had lost his seat at Bedford in 1966 and had been out of the House for eight years, during which he had served as British Ambassador in Paris and an EEC Commissioner in Brussels. He had therefore played no direct part in the Heath administration, but as an ex-minister had the advantage of appearing as a dark horse who had not been identified with recent policies. His major disadvantages were that he had not got a seat in Parliament and was largely unknown to the new generation of members of the parliamentary party, which made up something like a third of the potential voting force. He was also strongly committed to his responsibilities in Europe in the immediate future, particularly with the prospect of re-negotiation, a referendum and what might come after it.

Broadly speaking, the same section of the party who were interested in Sir Christopher as a candidate were also likely to be interested in Sir Keith Joseph. Both men were fairly right-wing and it was from the same group that their support might be expected to come. Sir Keith Joseph was a former fellow of All Souls College, Oxford and one of the outstanding intellects in Conservative politics. He had also proved himself an effective administrator as Minister for Housing and Local Government under Harold Macmillan, and Secretary of State for the Social Services under Edward Heath. He had the reputation of being one of the most original thinkers in politics and an extremely hard-working Minister, though it was felt to some extent that he had become too introverted and closely absorbed with the multitudinous duties of his own department to be as effective a force as he might have been in general terms in the Heath Cabinet. At all events, it had come as something of a surprise to· colleagues, when the party went into opposition at the beginning of 1974, to find Keith Joseph coming forward in a hair shirt proclaiming himself in public speeches a convinced but repentant monetarist. Although this emphasis on money supply had come, as he admitted, only late in the day, his formidable powers made him a persuasive advocate of the case for rigid control of printing further money in circumstances where the other main Tory propagandist of this principle, Enoch Powell, had put himself completely out of court on other grounds.

It is interesting, at this point, to consider what Powell's own position might have been in the autumn of 1974, if he had not put himself so totally at loggerheads with the majority of establishment feeling in his party, ending in the open revolt at the February election. Powell's intellectual gifts had originally gained him considerable regard in the party, which had increasingly been dissipated by his apparent willingness to embrace all manner of contentious causes in what seemed part of a personal animosity to Edward Heath. Although he continued to insist that he would live and die a member of the Conservative Party and that it was an honourable ambition to lead the party to which he had the right to aspire, his views on a multiplicity of issues appeared to be at variance with main-stream Conservative thinking. There were some who found his ideas on immigration, the Common Market and Northern Ireland extreme to the point of repugnance, but to the great majority of Conservatives it was his actions in deserting Wolverhampton South West just before the February election, and the party in both campaigns, that made him an inconceivable alternative despite his great gifts and his abilities as a publicist.

If the leadership was to be changed, the real problem seemed to be not only who the possible contenders might be but how the system as such was to be altered. Edward Heath himself was the first leader who had been elected under the new process of appointment which followed the retirement of Sir Alec Douglas-Home in 1965. This had initiated a choice on, if necessary, a preferential rate system on second ballot, by the whole body of Conservative Members. As such it had replaced effectively the old 'magic circle' system of consultation by the elder statesmen and the Whips which had led to the selection of Harold Macmillan in 1957 and Sir Alec himself in 1963. But there was still no effective term put upon the leader's right to occupy the office once he had been elected to that position by the parliamentary party and confirmed by the whole party as such. Unlike the parliamentary Labour Party which, under the terms of its constitution re-elects the leader every year when it is in opposition, there was no automatic process whereby Conservative members might reconsider or even challenge who the leader should be once he had been checked and confirmed in the first place. Having defeated Reggie Maudling and Enoch Powell in the succession to Sir Alec in 1965, no one had come forward at any stage until 1974 to suggest that Edward Heath should submit himself for re-election.

It was to resolve this situation that the executive of the 1922 went into a series of apparently agonising discussions immediately after the October election. Having met discreetly at Edward du Cann's home in Belgravia but come to no firm decision, they then proceeded to a system of more confidential consultation. Unfortunately this was blown wide open by the activity of an energetic journalist who found the whole body in private confabulation at du Cann's offices at Milk Street in the City of London. As a result they gained for themselves not only the unfortunate and rather comic soubriquet of the 'Milk Street Mafia' but also the impression that something was afoot in which they were involved. Meanwhile, although the right-wing-inclined Monday Club called on him to resign so that the party could revert to more Conservative principles, Edward Heath's own inner circles of friends and advisers were counselling him to sit tight and ride out the storm. While Harold Wilson, drawing on his election successes, appealed to the nation to support him in solving the problems which were facing his government the Tory party seemed to be willing to help him by tearing themselves to pieces.

Shaken in morale, uncertain as to which precise road they wanted to travel, they seemed to be equally uncertain as to whom they wished to lead them along their way. The period of the Heath Government from 1970 to 1974 had not done much to highlight the reputation of any of the individual ministers involved, with the possible exception of William Whitelaw. The death of Ian Macleod, the appointment of Lord Hailsham to the Woolsack and the temporary retirement of Reggie Maudling to the backbenches had removed three of its best-known members. Robert Carr, who had come to play a prominent role during the period of the Industrial Relations Act, was too closely identified with this controversial piece of legislation to seem a credible alternative to Edward Heath. On the Tuesday following the election *The Times* tentatively came to the conclusion that 'the possibility is that Mr Heath will go fairly quickly and that Mr Whitelaw will be elected to succeed him', but it added that this was by no means certain as the Conservative Party in Parliament were not yet at all sure whom they ought to choose. The rest of the press seemed equally uncertain though there was a certain amount of support for the suggestion that the effective contender against the existing leader might be Sir Keith Joseph. It was also generally acknowledged that neither Willie Whitelaw nor Jim Prior were likely to enter the contest unless Edward Heath chose to go of his own accord.

This he showed no signs of doing. Although he acknowledged his particular responsibility for maintaining the unity of the Conservative Party he went on television, in a ministerial broadcast in reply to Harold Wilson, and spoke of his continuing responsibility as leader of the Conservative Party and Leader of the Opposition to do all he could to hold Britain and Europe together. It was clearly in this role that he saw his function in the ensuing session of Parliament. It was an impressive performance and made clear that, whatever the events of the last week, his personal resolve to fight Wilson over the fundamentals of policy was not weakening nor had his nerve been unduly shaken. Equally, it was obvious that he must do something with regard to the party after their double electoral defeat. On 17th October, a week after the election, he wrote to Edward du Cann indicating that he would welcome discussions about the future with either the re-elected Executives of the 1922 Committee or that body as a whole, after the elections for a new Executive had taken place.

This would have the effect of postponing the main issue but only for a matter of a few weeks at the most. In the meantime Willie Whitelaw came out with a characteristically generous statement of support. 'My own admiration and support for Ted Heath as our leader is well known and does not waver, least of all in times of difficulty,' he wrote. 'I naturally accept that all members of the Conservative Party are entitled to their own views about the leadership of their party. Yet surely at this time of crisis, as Conservatives, our priority is clear; it is our nation first.'

Just how great this crisis had become was now increasingly clear as Harold Wilson turned from the euphoria of election success to meet the reality of the problems which were facing the economy and also the unity of his own party. If the Conservative Party had its problems, so did he. Faced with an increasingly overt demand from the by now increased number of left-wing members in the House for more rigorously Socialist policies he had to balance the grim state of the nation's finances against their demands for greatly increased public expenditure in certain specific sectors, in particular the extension of state control in industry. A number of his own ministers, including the veteran Labour backbencher Michael Foot, now promoted as Secretary for Employment, and the able, ambitious and energetic Anthony Wedgwood Benn as Secretary for Trade, were closely identified with this. While, in the meantime, the financial situation deteriorated to an alarming degree, he was likely to find himself faced with an ultimate crisis over either the implications of a Referendum on membership of the EEC or the need to reimpose some form of wages and incomes control, which had been taken off when his government came to power. In the present circumstances his inclination seemed to be to give the left its head as much as possible, in both Parliament and the constituency parties, so that Britain seemed to be likely to face a bout of highly Socialist legislation on education, medicine, industry and particularly tax over the ensuing months. Although the Tory party had not got enough strength in the House to do much to contain such controversial measures on its own, they were clearly going to need to put forward a coherent alternative.

One such blueprint was put forward at Birmingham as early as 19th October in the shape of a speech by Sir Keith Joseph. Although some of his colleagues might regard him as an introvert, he was prepared when necessary to enter into some highly controversial fields. Basically what he was talking about was the moral regeneration of the nation. In a vigorous appeal for politicians to think of something beside economics, he contended that we should all be concerned as a country with maintaining the family and fundamental ethical values. It was concern for their responsibilities in housing, health, education and care of the elderly which gave families themselves cohesion and purpose. All of this was perfectly straightforward, orthodox Conservative philosophy, even though the way in which it was spelt out seemed to be putting Sir Keith on record as a possible Tory challenger.

He went on, however, to cover a range of disconnected subjects in his general theme. Among these was a topic with which he had been deeply concerned as Secretary for Social Services, the battered baby syndrome and the cycle of deprivation. Here he made a direct reference to what he saw as the need for curbing population increase, especially among areas of high incidence of unwanted or emotionally unstable pregnancies among girls in the lower socio-economic classes (classes four and five) who were, he claimed, making less use of contraceptive facilities than other women did. Though controversial, such contentions were not particularly new. What was more unusual was their employment as part of a more generalised political argument in the course of a public speech. In the light of his position as a possible Conservative challenger, the press made Sir Keith's Birmingham speech into a nine-days' wonder.

The 19th October was a Saturday and over the weekend the Sunday papers and television, the Churches, the Family Planning Association, the Child Poverty Action Group, the sociologists and the politicians all had their say. Mr Tom Jackson of the Post Office Workers Union even saw the speech as the foundation stone for a sort of incipient fascism in this country. 'There are two things I am not clear about,' he was quoted as saying. 'The first is whether (Sir Keith) is going to employ veterinary surgeons to blow the contraceptive pill down the throats of the deserving poor, and how soon he is going to introduce thought police. He has quoted Orwell and this speech is like 1984.'

Even Sir Keith himself subsequently admitted that it was probably a 'naive mistake' to include the birth control comments in such a context. In fact the speech probably did more than anything else to put him out of the count as a prospective Conservative leader. Coupled with his previous speeches, particularly one at Preston during the election campaign on inflation, unemployment and money supply, it was clear that he was ready and willing to supply a much needed intellectual stimulus to the political scene. Although the Birmingham speech reiterated his desire to bring a sense of purpose to his party's deliberations, the way in which it was handled gave the Parliamentary party a warning as to the risks that it might be running if it chose Sir Keith as the leader. Probably what worried his colleagues most was the surprise which he showed at the speech being controversial at all.

When the House reassembled a few days later to take the oath, the pendulum seemed to be swinging back firmly in favour of Edward Heath. The majority of the existing Shadow Cabinet appeared to be giving him their support and he had the additional advantage of holding future appointments to the front bench in his own hand. Further, it was evident that the question of Europe was likely to loom very large both with Parliament and in the country as a whole during the next session, and here his expertise was second to none. With Soames in Brussels, Joseph seriously behind in the running and other possible contenders like Whitelaw and Prior willing to wait quietly until he made a decision, it appeared that he might be able to hold on by default.

Nevertheless, when the 1922 Committee met on Tuesday, 21st October there was still strong pressure from speakers for bringing up to date the whole process of electing the leader. Although most of these emphasised their personal regard for Edward Heath, the issue was formulated as to whether the leadership should be regarded as a freehold or a leasehold for its occupant, and if the latter, as one speaker put it, on what kind of lease should it be held?

When the new opposition front bench appointments were announced on 7th November, it was obvious that Heath was regarding these on a strictly back-to-business approach. The purpose of the new team was to fight Socialism in the House, just as it was the job of the party to fight it throughout the country. Willie Whitelaw was given special responsibility for the problem of devolution, as well as continuing as Chairman of the party. John Peyton, the witty, incisive member for Yeovil, was made shadow Leader of the House against the politically accident-prone Edward Short. Geoffrey Rippon, who had led the European negotiations during 1970–72, was appointed to succeed Sir Alec, who had gone back to the Lords, as shadow foreign secretary. A number of bright young men were promoted and Margaret Thatcher, who had been shadow housing and environment secretary in opposition and was a previous Secretary of State for Education, was switched to work with Robert Carr on Treasury matters, with special responsibility for financial legislation and public expenditure.

Although she had in fact had her own departmental responsibilities for a number of years, this transfer was in no sense felt to be a demotion, but rather as an indication of how seriously the Tories were taking the forthcoming battle on fiscal and particularly on tax matters. As *The Times* rather majestically put it: 'It is widely expected that Mr Heath has decided to double-back his shadow appointments to cover the Treasury by retaining Mr Carr as Shadow Chancellor but reinforcing him with Mrs Thatcher, a rising Conservative star, as full-rank specialist in finance and taxation. Mrs Thatcher could well prove to be the first woman Chancellor of the Exchequer if her reputation in the party and the House continues to grow.' Another popular appointment was that of the extremely able Norman St John Stevas, who had been Margaret Thatcher's number two at Education during the last years of the Heath government, to take on full responsibility for this subject as well as reassuming responsibility for the arts.

In a hard-hitting speech, on the day that these appointments were made, to the Institute of Directors conference in London, the new Shadow Treasury spokesman made clear her reasons for her deep distrust as to the way in which Socialist economic policy was developing.

'The present difficulties in which many companies find themselves,' she said, 'are undoubtedly being used by left-wing groups to justify a further measure of state control. Little attempt is made to analyse either the cause of the problems or to consider the administrative difficulties at the government end if ever-increasing duties and decisions are formally placed on ministers.

'Last year industry paid £2,245 million in corporation tax. This year the estimate is £3,265 million. There have been various comments in Parliament that industry is asking for money. The reality is that if the government had not taken so much out, it would not need to put so much back in.

'The fact is that we owe in large measure the increase in both individual and collective prosperity since the war to the private enterprise system. And yet it has come under constant political attack. Our political opponents, whether they are in government in opposition, never cease to preach their beliefs about the economy and the case for more state control, while we have too often assumed the case for private enterprise instead of arguing it.

'The economic well-being and standard of living of the country depend largely on the performance of the private sector. I hope that within the coming few years, with or without legislation, companies will do everything possible to ensure that employees at every level feel themselves to be a part of the company and identify themselves with its success. Some companies have already made excellent progress in this direction, not because they have been pushed by the politicians but because it is good for the company, its people and therefore for the country.'

The views which the speaker expressed were very close to her own basic philosophy, and her means of expression was typically downright. It seemed a happy augury of what might be for Margaret Thatcher a difficult but rewarding period of work.

With the re-election in due course of Edward du Cann and the other members of the 1922 Executive, the decks were clear for Edward Heath to take some steps about the question of the leadership. At what point, if he ever had considered himself a candidate, du Cann decided to rule himself out of the stakes, is not clear, but when Heath came to a full meeting of the 1922 Committee on 14th November it was as an important functionary of the Parliamentary party and not as a potential rival that du Cann received him. Two immediate problems were involved. One was whether the position of leader should now be made subject to some regular method of confirmation while the party was in opposition. The other was the question of Heath's own continuation in the role. He agreed to initiate discussions with du Cann, with Willie Whitelaw as party chairman, with Lord Carrington as leader in the Lords and with Sir John Taylor, the chairman of the National Union as to how the procedure for appointing the leader should be revised. In his speech to the '22 he stressed the continuing need for party unity and was given a friendly reception. He accepted that there was no such thing as a 'freehold' as far as the job was concerned and suggested that a review committee should get on with evolving suitable procedures as soon as possible.

There is no doubt that the Conservative Party owes a great deal to Edward Heath for the quiet and efficient way that he continued, both in Parliament and at speaking engagements up and down the country, to carry on its business during this difficult period. He personally came out of the ordeal with considerable dignity, when under obvious pressure. Although deep feelings were involved in the discussons, it was obvious that what was really at stake was not just his personal future or who should lead the party during the next session, but what sort of image of Conservatism should be evolved at a time that was probably more vital to the party than any other since the war.

As so often in a difficult situation, the party turned to Sir Alec Douglas-Home, now Lord Home of the Hirsel, as its elder statesman, to advise it. He agreed to undertake the chairmanship of a committee to consider the question of elections for the leadership and he undertook to report by Christmas.

In the meantime some light relief was provided by the temporary re-emergence of Enoch Powell in Conservative circles. Now a United Ulster Unionist Member of Parliament, he addressed a Young Conservative meeting at Eastbourne, where he attacked all his previous colleagues who had continued to support the last Conservative government. In draconian terms, he accused them of allowing themselves to become politically corrupted by being wedded to office and being so frightened by the loss of its emoluments and appurtenances that they were driven into doing the wrong thing rather than face a period in the wilderness. It was a speech heavy with weighty periods, but it probably served to convince most people that the chances of any immediate reconciliation between the party and its best-known maverick were slimmer than ever and that the gap was becoming even deeper than it had been.

Meanwhile a new and totally different name began to be mentioned for the leadership, that of Margaret Thatcher. Though she herself was prepared to discount the suggestion when it was first made, on the grounds that the electorate might not be ready for a woman leader and that she had only so far held one of the main offices of state (education), a number of her Parliamentary colleagues thought otherwise. Although, when she was first mentioned, the bookies, who were beginning to offer odds on a possible leadership contest, had her at an outside price of 50 to 1, within the House of Commons itself groups of members began to consider the idea seriously and to like it. Unlike Edward du Cann and Willie Whitelaw she was not tied by holding existing office in the party hierarchy. Though she was regarded at first sight as being of the right it was not thought that she would allow herself to be caught in a doctrinaire stance as Sir Keith Joseph had done. As a member of the Heath Cabinet she was known to have had a mind of her own and was suspected of having been by no means blindly in favour of all its policies. In addition she was attractive to look at with a strong personality, but—and it remained a big but—she was a woman. A number of people might like the idea, but whether they were prepared to act on it remained a very different question.

One who was prepared to do so was John Gorst, the member for Hendon North and one of the younger members who had come in in 1970. Broadcasting on *The World at One* he put the case for Margaret Thatcher with some force: 'First and foremost, the leader of the Conservative Party must be someone who is modern, compassionate and dedicated to Conservative principles . . . Margaret Thatcher is all of those things.' It was an enthusiastic testimonial but some journalists were prepared to play it down on the basis that they had neighbouring constituencies (both in the London Borough of Barnet) and that Gorst was acting out of personal enthusiasm for someone whose work he particularly admired.

She was certainly adding to her reputation by her performances in the House and in Committee on Denis Healey's interim budget. In a devastating attack, winding up for the opposition on the evening of 14th November, she charged the Chancellor with failing to tell the nation what really lay ahead and of seeking to blind them with complications and statistics. The people, she said, were ready for sacrifices, the Chancellor was not. He had opted for sacrifice by instalment, first an increase on petrol, later price increases from the nationalised industries, later still, no doubt, increases in rates and taxes the following spring. Both the country and the Chancellor himself would in due course come to regret that he had done so little to prepare them for the realities of the situation. It was an extremely effective speech and she was lucky to have that moment to make it to show her abilities, but she equally knew how to make the most of her opportunities.

Despite the mention of Margaret Thatcher, the most likely possibilities seemed still to be either that Edward Heath would remain where he was or, if he did go, that the Tory establishment would rally round Willie Whitelaw as his successor. If the Douglas-Home proposals did evolve a system which led to a change, it seemed that the party would probably opt to play safe and that in every likelihood meant Whitelaw.

The Douglas-Home recommendations were in fact available in the third week of December. When they were published, not only did the method of election proposed appear to be extremely complicated ('a Byzantine constitution designed by the Abbé Sieyes', one distinguished political journalist called them) but it seemed that they were most likely to favour a continuance of the status quo.

Annual elections for the leader were proposed at the beginning of each new session of Parliament (ie once a year in effect), the voting to be by the whole of the Parliamentary party in the House of Commons, after consultation with the constituencies and the Conservative peers had shown their general preference. If necessary, three ballots were to be held. If on the first ballot a candidate received an overall majority of the votes cast plus 15% more than the runner-up of the number of votes entitled to be polled (as opposed to the previous system of a similar lead on the number of votes actually given), *he* (it is interesting that this was the word actually used in the document) would be elected.

If not, a second ballot would be held one week later. The original nominations would be held void and any of the first lot of candidates, or any new ones, could be nominated. On this ballot if a successful candidate got an overall majority, he was in. If this did not happen, then the three candidates who had received the most votes would automatically go forward for a poll two days later. On this third ballot the members would have to indicate their first and second choice and, by elimination of the candidate who got the smallest number of votes, these would be re-distributed on their indicated second preferences between the other two, one of whom was bound to have an overall majority.

Even to read it sounds a fairly breathless exercise. When Members of Parliament and political commentators had recovered from their original reaction to the complexity of this piece of machinery, they began to weigh up what its practical implications would be. First, and in general terms, the advantage seemed to lie in favour of the existing leader, who would have the opportunity to consolidate his votes on the second ballot and make the most of his built-in advantage. If he could hold off his opponents on the second count and hold his vote, he had a good chance of winning on the third round. The second and third ballots would therefore only be significant if there was a substantial amount of diplomatic voting or if a powerful challenger appeared to take the lead the first time round.

Secondly, what did this mean in terms of the candidates likely to stand? Edward Heath was certain to do so and had still got a substantial amount of rapport in the House of Commons and a lot of influential followers in the constituency parties and the House of Lords. In 1965 his initial vote had given him a firm advantage over Reggie Maudling and Enoch Powell, and a fair number of his original supporters were still there and had been added to by newer MPs closely associated with him like Douglas Hurd and John Macgregor, both former Heath aides who had come in in February 1974. The basis of the Tory establishment were certainly likely still to support him and this included a majority of his previous cabinet, including Whitelaw and Prior who would certainly not stand against him on the first ballot. Margaret Thatcher announced that she would stand, for reasons which she later gave in an interview with Brian Connell. 'I heard that Keith Joseph was not going to run against Ted. Someone had to. I said to Keith, "If you are not, I shall." There was no hesitation, there was no doubt, there has been no doubt since. It might have put me on the back benches for life, or out, I did not know. But the one thing I seemed to have was the power to make a decision when a decision had to be made.'

Although she was subject to criticism in some quarters for coming forward at all ('rocking the boat' and 'personal ambition' a few party loyalists groaned) it is interesting to see how totally disinterested her decision to stand actually was. 'Someone had to stand.' There was a problem, she felt, to be solved for the party and for the country. She herself no longer believed, and there were others who felt like her, that Ted Heath could command the across-the-board support to do this. At any rate it had to be put to the test. If no one else of suitable standing was willing to be a contestant against the former leader, she had to.

Ever since her name had first been mentioned as a possible candidate, her ideas and her utterances had been subject to continual scrutiny by her colleagues and by the press. She nearly suffered an early set-back when an article written in a totally different context advising couples who were preparing for retirement was given extensive publicity. What in fact she had said was to cite stock-piling a limited amount of tinned foods and preserves, with a certain amount of consumer durables for long-term use as a hedge against inflation. Although some economic pundits agitated that this was actually encouraging inflation, it was a perfectly sensible piece of advice, which she admitted that she herself followed for her own family. Despite suggestions from some of the dottier flat-earthers that she was an anti-social hoarder pursuing her own form of siege economy, the whole thing died a nine-days' wonder.

Much more serious was the suggestion that she had little or no experience in the fields of foreign politics or defence, and her argument that she had made regular overseas visits and contacts as Secretary for Education did not seem to be particularly persuasive. On the other hand she had shown in a number of different fields that she was a quick learner and it was a moot point in the 1970s anyway whether the British people were more concerned about having an expert in foreign affairs as prime minister or someone who knew their own and their families' problems at home at first hand. Although Europe was clearly important, it was the impact of the Community on the lives of ordinary people in this country, rather than the formal treaty obligations which many of them did not really understand, which seemed to loom largest here. Nevertheless, Edward Heath had an undoubted plus in his world-wide reputation as an international statesman.

The suggestion that she was lukewarm on Europe she repudiated angrily. In a statement which she later released on the eve of the second ballot she was to pay tribute to Edward Heath's achievement in leading Britain into the Community and she said unequivocally: 'This torch must be picked up and carried by whoever is chosen to succeed him. The commitment to European partnership is one which I fully serve.'

The first ballot was scheduled for Tuesday, 4th February 1975. Three names were eventually proposed, the third being that of Hugh Fraser, the extremely agreeable member for Stafford and Stone. Fraser, who is married to the well-known writer and television personality Antonia Fraser, was something of a surprise candidate since he had not himself held office since 1964 when he had been Minister for the RAF. He was a man of strong principle, a High Tory with a mind of his own and a Catholic. He was also very well liked in the House of Commons though whether personal friendships were likely to account for more than a handful of votes in a contest of this kind remained to be seen. By entering the race he was unlikely to get more than a protest vote on the first ballot, but could provide a focus for some of the more traditional Tory members who had found themselves increasingly in conflict with Heath but had not yet got used to the idea of a woman as leader of the party.

In a speech to her own constituency association on the eve of the election, Margaret Thatcher made it clear exactly where she stood: 'In the desperate situation which faces Britain today, our party needs the support of all who value the traditional ideals of Toryism: compassion and concern for the individual and his freedom; opposition to excessive state power; the right of the enterprising, the hardworking and the thrifty to succeed and to reap the rewards of success and pass some of them on to their children; encouragement of that infinite diversity of choice that is an essential of freedom—the defence of widely distributed private property against the Socialist state; the right of a man to work without oppression by either employer or union boss.

'There is a widespread feeling in the country that the Conservative Party has not defended these ideals explicitly and toughly enough, so that Britain is set on a course towards inevitable Socialist mediocrity. That course must not only be halted, it must be reversed.'

Voting took place at the House of Commons between 12.00 am and 3.30 pm. Contrary to previous speculation, when the result was announced Margaret Thatcher had won by a considerable margin with 130 votes to Edward Heath's 119, Hugh Fraser receiving 16 votes. Immediately, and with characteristic dignity, Heath announced that he would not stand in a further ballot and passed the functions of leader over *pro tem* to Robert Carr. The way was now open for any of his previous supporters to try their chances on a second ballot. In the end there were no less than five candidates on this. In addition to Margaret Thatcher, Willie Whitelaw, Jim Prior, John Peyton and Sir Geoffrey Howe, an ex-Solicitor General and Minister of Consumer Protection, stood.

Margaret Thatcher herself was reported as saying that she did not expect to win on the first round. Apart from the fact that feeling in the constituencies was known to have rallied round Edward Heath, his candidacy had been endorsed by many senior personalities in the party. She had imagined that feeling against a woman candidate would weigh more strongly against her than it did, and that there would be a greater use of tactical voting for various reasons. In fact there was only a small handful of abstentions, some of these accidental through absence abroad, on the first vote.

She had now, however, achieved a position of considerable strength and, as her campaign manager Airey Neave, the member for Abingdon, reported, could feel quietly confident without taking anything for granted. The fact that she had had the courage to come forward on the first ballot certainly enormously increased her standing. Someone who had had the strength to stand against and beat Heath in these circumstances was of the calibre, many members felt, to beat Wilson or any other Labour leader and to win very effectively. In the first instance most of her supporters had turned to her on a personal basis, including one or two senior members like Sir Keith Joseph and a considerable number of the younger ones. Airey Neave, an old Parliamentary hand with a distinguished record of escapes from Colditz during the war, had run her campaign efficiently and without fuss as opposed to the rather brasher tactics of Peter Walker who had managed the campaign for Edward Heath. Now there was a widespread swing to her in the constituency parties as well. The summary of constituency opinion submitted to the 1922 Executive on the day before the second ballot and relayed to members showed that feeling in the constituencies was two to one in her favour as against Willie Whitelaw standing anywhere at all. Even then, however, it was thought that she might have to go to a third ballot to get a necessary majority.

During the period leading up to the second vote there were a number of opportunities for the press and television to compare the style of the contestants. Slightly unwisely, Willie Whitelaw allowed himself to be photographed in a rather uncharacteristic pose, washing-up in the kitchen of his London home. Both he and Margaret Thatcher appeared, by long-standing invitation, at the Young Conservative Annual Conference at Eastbourne over the week-end. The YCs, who had previously appeared to favour Edward Heath in the main, gave them each a boisterous welcome but undoubtedly the advantage lay with Margaret Thatcher. Fortunately for her, by terms of the originally arranged programme, Willie Whitelaw was restricted to answering at a questions and answer session while she was down to speak in reply to a debate on the economy. This she did with considerable effect.

'We want a mixed economy but what else do we want?' she asked. 'I believe we should judge people on their merits and not on their background; I believe that a person who is prepared to work hard should receive greater rewards and keep them after tax. I believe we should back workers not shirkers; that it is not only permissible but praiseworthy to want to benefit your own family by your own efforts; that liberty must never be confused with licence, and that you cannot have liberty without a just law, impartially administered.' This was fighting talk of a kind which had been largely absent on Conservative platforms in recent months and the Young Conservatives loved it.

On the Monday evening the four other candidates appeared on the BBC's *Panorama* programme. None of them did much to improve their chances greatly. Margaret Thatcher had also been asked to appear but had decided not to on the basis that by recording her speech before transmission, as each of the contestants was asked to, she would not be able to reply to any comments which were made on filmed extracts from her Eastbourne speech. Although she had probably nothing to worry about in the circumstances and was criticised for her decision at the time, it was probably tactically the right one.

The voting on the second ballot took place in Committee Room 14. Even Margaret Thatcher's most enthusiastic supporters, like John Gorst, William Shelton and Joan Hall, a former Yorkshire member who was acting as an extra aide during the election, cannot have been prepared for quite such an overwhelming vote of confidence. As against 146 votes which were recorded for her, Willie

Whitelaw had 79, Jim Prior and Sir Geoffrey Howe 19 each and John Peyton 11. She had obtained a clear majority over all the other candidates by a clear margin of 7 votes, in an election in which practically every vote had been cast.

Airey Neave brought the news to his room at the Commons where she had been waiting with a group of close supporters. After a brief moment of emotion, her reaction was characteristic: 'Thank God it is decisive,' was her only comment. 'We have got a lot to do. Now we must get down to work at once.'

After writing notes of sympathy to the other contestants, her first job was to face the world's press. In her initial press conference as leader of the opposition, she met a barrage of questions with good humour and a great deal of aplomb. Although it must have been a gruelling day, she appeared cool and remarkably unruffled.

'To me,' she said, 'it is like a dream come true that the next name in the list Macmillan, Home and Heath is Margaret Thatcher. Each has brought his own style of leadership and stamp of greatness to his task and I shall take on the task with humility and dedication. . . . It is important to me that this prize has been won in open electoral contest with four other potential leaders. I know they will be disappointed but I hope we shall soon be back working together as colleagues for the nation in which we all believe. There is much to do and I hope you will allow me to do it thoughtfully and well.'

Asked if she would like to provide more opportunities for women, she answered: 'The first thing to do is to get more women into Parliament, then we shall be less conspicuous.' In reply to a long-winded subsidiary question from a male journalist, she replied in a characteristic flash: 'You chaps don't like a direct answer. Men like long, rambling, waffling answers.'

Then she went off quietly to celebrate with her husband and family but was back in her place at the House on the Finance Bill Committee later the same evening.

Equally characteristically, the Conservative Party rallied to her, whether they had been her supporters in the voting or not. Feeling was summed up by Edward du Cann in a television broadcast that night: 'We have got a new and rather exciting leader. Mrs Thatcher will make the Tory Party distinctive. Her election signals a new start, recreating, refreshing and reinvigorating.'

All four of the other contestants on the second ballot agreed to serve with her, Willie Whitelaw as deputy leader, Sir Geoffrey Howe as Shadow Chancellor and Jim Prior and John Peyton in senior posts. In addition her shadow cabinet was to be strengthened by the return to the front bench of Reggie Maudling as shadow foreign secretary. Edward Heath had refused any shadow appointment and chose to go to the backbenches, though he sent her a message of congratulations and good will.

Understandably, reaction on the Socialist side veered from apprehensive to hostile. One or two Labour members were faintly apologetic that it should be the Conservatives who had been the first party to choose a woman as their leader. Joel Barnett, the Chief Secretary to the Treasury, gave her a courteous welcome when she returned to the Finance Committee immediately after her election. 'If you go on looking as attractive as you do tonight,' he remarked, 'it will be a great benefit to the House.'

When asked what she felt about facing Harold Wilson across the floor of the House, she had replied at her preliminary press conference: 'About the same as he feels about facing me, I imagine.' When the confrontation took place for the first time the following afternoon at Prime Minister's question time, he was certainly not very much at ease with the situation. After offering his congratulations he went on to say: 'From a study of her speeches I have formed the opinion that there may be a deep gulf between the Right Honourable Lady and myself.' This remark was greeted by Conservative cheers.

Then with one of the extempore quips that are sometimes an embarrassing feature of his repertoire, he went on to make play with the fact that the normal place for consultation between the two front bench leaders in the chamber was the small and rather dark area behind the Speaker's chair. 'I look forward to meetings behind your chair, Mr Speaker, and to the informality which, judging from my experience of her three predecessors, the intimacy of such meetings makes possible.' The remark got a laugh but Margaret Thatcher was not amused, and it was a quip for which he was to pay dearly in debate during the next few months.

A more dignified occasion was her meeting with Conservative members, peers and constituency officers, when she was formally installed as leader of the party the following week. In proposing her election, Lord Hailsham said that he did not believe that any previous Tory leader had taken office in time of peace when the country was faced with more immediate perils, or when the general public had been less alive to the reality of the dangers with which it was faced. In replying, Margaret Thatcher spoke with equal frankness and deep concern for the future of Britain.

'We know well,' she said, 'that there are complex issues which we face now, some of them new, some of them being experienced to a degree, like inflation, which we have never experienced before, some of them making great demands on world resources, some of them requiring changes in world institutions.

'We must consider all these things and find policies to deal with the complex nature of society before us, both its complex nature nationally and internationally. We must have policies for the future. We must be properly equipped for the task.

c

'But if we need purpose and vision, we also need a third thing and that is presentation. It is no good having a first-class product unless people know about it. And they won't know about it unless we tell them.

'The price of failure is heavy. The heritage which our forefathers bequeathed us must be renewed and passed on to future generations. To the fulfilment of that task and in honour of all our previous leaders I pledge all my strength, loyalty and determination.'

Margaret Thatcher had come a long way to become, at the age of 49, the first woman leader of a great national party in the country, first lady of the House, and the potential prime minister. Remarkable as her career had already been, considerable as had been her achievements, she was going to have to shoulder burdens heavier than those which had faced practically any previous statesman, for which she would need all her courage, her coolness, her determination and her human qualities. It was a moment for which she had unconsciously been prepared by all her previous life.

2

Enter Margaret Thatcher

When Margaret Thatcher became the Leader of the Conservative Party no other part of the country could have been more jubilant than the small Lincolnshire town of Grantham. It was there that Hilda Margaret Roberts was born on 13th October, 1925 in the flat above a shop in North Parade, where her father ran a business as a sub-postmaster and grocer.

Alfred Roberts was in many ways a remarkable man. He was a native of Ringstead, near Wellingborough, in Northamptonshire, where his father ran a business as a shoe manufacturer. The family originally had Welsh origins and his mother, from whom he inherited a strong feeling for music and for words, was Irish. He originally hoped to be a teacher, but as happened so often with the Northamptonshire shoe trade at the beginning of the century, his father lost his money and he was taken away from school at the earliest opportunity to earn his living. A place was found for him as an assistant to a grocer at Grantham and by the age of twenty-one he was made a manager. In 1917 he married Beatrice Ethel Stevenson, whose parents came from Grantham, and a couple of years later they bought their own business at North Parade, subsequently branching out with a second shop in another part of the town.

Grantham in many ways is the epitome of provincial England. Situated on the old Great North Road, 110 miles north of London, it lies between the arable country of Kesteven to the east and the grasslands of the vale of Belvoir to the west. It is a town of mostly red brick houses, dominated by the grey stone tower and spire of St Wulfram's, one of the great medieval churches in which this part of the country excels. It developed rapidly during the nineteenth century, with the population, which in the 1930s was just on 20,000, doubling over the hundred years preceding this. An important centre for agricultural engineering, it also had a busy Saturday market and served the farming community for miles round. Its great glory is the King's School, a grammar school re-endowed by Edward VI, where Sir Isaac Newton, whose statue stands proudly in the middle of Grantham where it is occasionally decorated by local wags with apples, was educated. It also has an excellent girls' school, the Kesteven and Grantham School, which is of more recent origin.

Margaret Thatcher herself has acknowledged how important a part her background has played in her upbringing. 'I always believe,' she wrote, 'that I was very lucky to have been brought up in a small town with a great sense of friendliness and voluntary service.' Being a member of a close family was also extremely important to her. She was a second child, her sister Muriel being four years older. The house in which they lived, which was a combination of shops knocked together to form a larger one, is still standing and the business still bears her father's name though he retired in 1960, ten years before he died.

Alfred Roberts was a tall, thin, naturally distinguished-looking man. He always wore glasses for short-sight but beneath these had what his eldest daughter describes as the bluest eyes she has ever seen apart from Elizabeth Taylor's. He was methodical, kindly and extremely neat. Miss Young-Jamieson, who was secretary for the local Home Guard during the war, remembers the infinite pains he took to see that her large daily official post was correctly sent off to the right parts of the county. On another level, Mrs Standish Harris, who lived nearby when her stepfather was posted as a regular RAF officer to Cranwell, remembers how kind he was to her and her small sister when they took their pennies in to choose sweets in the shop. Perhaps because his own schooling had been cut off earlier than he had wanted, he was a great reader and education mattered a lot to him. He was later to be a governor of both the principal Grantham schools and Chairman for a number of years of the Kesteven Girls School, on the board of which he remained to the time of his death.

Mrs Roberts was a less bookish person than her husband but, like him, had a great fund of natural kindness and was intensely proud of running a tidy house and keeping a happy home for her family. When he became Mayor of the borough, she was an excellent Mayoress, concerned for the people of Grantham and interested in everybody she met. As her husband put it, in officially accepting the office, their aim was to serve, together, the whole community.

Public service was very important to the whole family. Two years after his eldest daughter's birth, Alfred Roberts was elected to the Council as a candidate proposed by the local Chamber of Trade and Ratepayers' Association. He was to serve on the Council for 25 years, nine of them as an alderman, including his year as Mayor in 1945–46. He was a President of the Grantham Chamber of Trade, an enthusiastic Rotarian who held all the major offices in his club, a director of the Grantham Building Society and the local Trustee Savings Bank and Chairman of the National Savings movement in the neighbourhood. Although in the First World War, after volunteering for the army, he was medically rejected after only three days on account of his eyesight, he played an enthusiastic part in the Second World War as a chief welfare officer for Civil Defence.

It is difficult to write about a career of this sort, dedicated to the local community, without making it sound priggish but, talking to people in Grantham who knew Alfred Roberts well, it is very clear that priggish is exactly what he was not. There are probably three principal reasons for this. As an individual he had a quiet but very strong sense of humour. Like his wife he was possessed of a very strong religious faith. They worshipped for years at the Finkin Street Methodist Church, where there is now a lectern dedicated by his family to his memory, and he was a sought-after local preacher and a trustee of some ten other churches on the Lincolnshire circuit. There was also, despite a belief in tradition, something of a radical about him.

When he was made Mayor, the *Grantham Journal* paid him a remarkable tribute. 'Although his opinions have on occasions been at variance with those held by other sections of the community,' they write, 'he is a man who holds to them and is respected for the forthright and open stand which he takes in public affairs.' He had in fact been offered the mayoralty five years previously but had refused it then owing to pressure of other commitments. Two years later, in 1943, he became the youngest alderman on the council. At the mayor-making in July 1945, his proposer and seconder spoke of him as a 'tower of strength' and praised his forthrightness and unchallengeable integrity.

Because he stood as an independent in a happier and less political era of local government, there have been speculations in the press since his daughter became leader as to precisely where his political affiliations did lie, and it has been suggested that his sympathies were with the Liberals rather than the Conservatives. This seems on the face of it, highly unlikely since he spoke for Margaret Thatcher during her campaign in Dartford in 1950, and she was encouraged to take an active part in party politics in national elections from quite an early age. In the 1945 general election, she was described by the *Grantham Journal* as taking an active part in the campaign for Squadron Leader G. A. Worth, the local Tory candidate, and 'with her father's gift of oratory . . . the presence of a young woman of the age of nineteen with such decided convictions has been no small factor in influencing the women's votes in the division.' Her father was certainly an outstanding speaker. David Wood, who is now the political editor of *The Times* but was originally a junior reporter on the *Grantham Journal*, can remember the fair and clear way that Alderman Roberts, as Chairman of the Finance Committee, took business through council meetings.

Both Mr and Mrs Roberts loved music, though Mrs Roberts was probably even more musical than her husband. Under their guidance Finkin Street Church became a well-known centre for local musical events. Both the girls were encouraged to learn the piano and Margaret took part in the piano competitions at the 1939 Grantham Musical Festival. A number of well-known singers came down to Finkin Street and Muriel Roberts, now Mrs Cullen, can remember, years afterwards, the celebrated soprano Jennifer Vyvian coming up to her when shopping in a well-known London store and asking whether she was the Roberts's daughter and speaking affectionately of her parents and her visits to Grantham. With her parents, however, music meant classical music and she can also remember with relief her parents going out to Rotary Ladies Nights when she and her sister could listen to Henry Hall or other dance bands on the radio without outraging their elders' musical susceptibilities. The girls also had an old tin gramophone on which they would giggle together over records like 'Coming through the Rye' and 'The Laughing Policeman'.

Both of them went to Huntingtower Road Elementary School, a recently built school about a mile from their parents' home and from there to the Kesteven and Grantham Girls' School. Although Margaret won a scholarship to the grammar school, it was a difficult position financially for the Roberts family since a considerable proportion of their income went on paying school fees, but they never doubted for one moment that it was worth it. They were lucky in that the Kesteven Girls School was an extremely good one with a reputation that stretched far beyond the immediate confines of Lincolnshire. For a couple of years after she went there Margaret came under the original founder and headmistress, the diminutive but formidable Miss Gladys Williams, who retired when Margaret was thirteen, and she was later much influenced by three teachers, Miss Gillis, the next headmistress, Miss Clegg, who taught her French and Miss Kay, the senior chemistry mistress.

It was Miss Gillis who encouraged her father to let her take the now celebrated elocution lessons. The reason was not, as has been suggested, to rid her of a Lincolnshire accent, of which both girls at this point had attractive traces, but because Grantham had recently started its own Eistedfodd in which the girls were encouraged to take part in the speaking competitions. She was therefore sent to be taught the clearness and precision of speech which has made her one of the most easily understood and attractive speakers in the contemporary House of Commons.

She was a hard-working and attentive pupil at school and quick to absorb facts, but it was also what she learnt at home that mattered. It was an extremely happy home and she had a great deal of respect and affection for both her parents. Everybody who speaks of him says that Alfred Roberts was an extraordinarily nice man and it was easy for him to instil into his daughters the principles on which his own life was based, self-reliance, courage and a concern for others.

The four-year age gap between her and her sister meant that Margaret tended to make her own friends, although, on account of her working ability, she was generally the youngest in her class. She also became an enthusiastic hockey player and became the youngest girl in the school ever to be selected for the hockey first eleven and its youngest-ever captain. It was natural to her to be extremely competitive in everything she did. Although she was intellectually ambitious and serious-minded there was also a good deal of fun about her and it was perhaps for this reason that other girls did not resent either her application or her success. While Muriel had gone on the general studies side, her sister opted for science, and chemistry in particular, not necessarily because she was of a peculiarly scientific bent of mind but because she had set her heart on Oxford and it was easier for a girl to get to that university if she was going to read a scientific subject. She had inherited her parents' neatness and in particular her father's clarity of mind, and it made it easy for her to assimilate and marshal her facts in this field.

Oxford, however, presented specific problems. The university had introduced, in war-time conditions, a shortened course for a two-year degree. If she waited until 1944 she would only go up for two years. If she took her entrance immediately which would get her there for the full three years, she would have to take Latin to enter, which she had not done since she started to specialise in scientific subjects. Miss Gillis was adamant that no-one could cram five years of Latin into the one year available for her. Margaret was equally determined that she could. She persuaded her father to let her try and a Mr Waterhouse was found to give her special coaching. Typically, when she came to take the exam, she came out first in it.

She also sat for a scholarship for Somerville and here she encountered real disappointment. There was only one award available in the group which she sat, and although she ended up equal first on the papers and the interview the other girl had waited on for an extra year to try the scholarship and it was her last chance of getting in. The college authorities decided to give her the award in the circumstances and Margaret Roberts was given a bursary which covered the cost of her books and equipment but not her tuition or residence fees. It was a set-back after having achieved so much, but Alfred Roberts rose to the occasion. He had made up his mind that his daughter must be given the chance to take up the opportunities which her abilities had opened up for her, and although it was bound to be a strain he decided that she should take her place at Somerville and that he would pay the costs. The emphasis which he placed on education was to have a considerable influence on her mind when she later became Secretary of State for Education and Science and fought for the best opportunities for schooling for young people.

It also weighed with her in her determination to make the most of her chances and in a strong feeling that girls should be given every opportunity to use their educational facilities in after life. Years later, speaking at Spilsby Grammar School in Lincolnshire in 1961, she was to say: 'It is wrong to contend that because a girl will get married she does not need the best possible training. Girls should not only take qualifications—they should try to do some part-time work after marriage.' For her it was a lasting belief that people should, wherever possible, try to achieve fulfilment and that a bright girl or woman was only going to feel fulfilled if she could put her brain to its best use.

Although going up to Oxford made a break in her full-time links with Grantham, it did not mean an end to her connection with her home or with her home town. Her sister had already qualified as a physiotherapist and had been appointed to a hospital in Blackpool. Both girls came home when they could, however, to play their part during their father's year of mayoralty. It was the year of the victory celebrations after the war had ended and an outstandingly successful one for Alderman and Mrs Roberts. Not only was he much concerned with obtaining new industries and job openings for the town and for servicemen returning from the war, but he also became closely involved with particular post-war problems such as housing and the setting-up of efficient local social services. It was an excellent ground training in practical politics for Margaret, but it also stressed for her what was to become one of her abiding principles, the need for voluntary service in the community. Not only did she concern herself particularly with the care of old people but she also instituted with some of her friends a kind of 'Any Questions' forum which went round to provide entertainment in the villages at a time when there was not much amusement to be had, with petrol rationing, for people in this part of the country.

Another important side-effect of her father's year as Mayor was that it introduced her to the work of the courts. Grantham, as an ancient borough which had been incorporated since 1463, had its own court of quarter sessions presided over by a Recorder, and one of the duties of the Mayor was to sit with him in court as an *ex-officio* justice. The then Recorder was Norman Winning, an able lawyer, with a busy practice on the Midland Circuit. Accompanying her father to court she became fascinated with the logic and precision of legal matters and, although she continued to study science, it was probably from this period and from her conversations with Winning that her eventual determination to become a barrister, if the opportunity arose, was born.

Meanwhile, she threw herself heart and soul into Oxford. Although when she went up the university was subject to wartime restrictions, during her second two years it became more like itself again with people coming back from war service and an outstandingly able generation of younger undergraduates coming up.

After wartime and the confines of a small town like Grantham, Oxford must have had an enormous amount to offer Margaret Roberts. She threw herself with enthusiasm into college activities and into the social and intellectual life of the university. She joined and sang with the Oxford Bach Choir. She continued to make a name for herself as an accomplished speaker. Strangely, although women had sat in Parliament for nearly a quarter of a century at that time, the Union, which modelled itself in other ways on Westminster, was still not open to them. Although some members, including the Honourable Anthony Wedgwood Benn of New College were campaigning for their admission, it was to remain a closed shop for a number of years. Perhaps, then as now, his advocacy of a cause proved counter-productive in a number of quarters.

Women could, however, play a leading part in the political organisations and she became in rapid succession Secretary, Treasurer and the third ever girl to become Chairman of the Oxford University Conservative Association.

Politics had come to play an increasingly important part in her life even before she left Grantham. Sir John Tilney, for many years the Conservative member for Liverpool (Wavertree), met her first when she was only seventeen because his sister, Mrs Brace, who lived at Gonnerby on the outskirts of Grantham, was a local councillor and knew the Roberts family well. He was struck even when she was that age by her ability and the enthusiasm which she showed when she talked about political matters. Curiously, nearly twenty-five years later she and Lady Tilney were to be co-chairwomen of the Women's National Commission.

An undergraduate contemporary who was very impressed with her ability was Sir Edward Boyle, later a Conservative minister and now Vice-Chancellor of Leeds University. Lord Boyle, as he now is, was a fellow committee member in OUCA. She was, he thought, always good value socially and had a great capacity for enjoying herself. She was always ready to throw herself into an occasion and liked taking part in things. She was extremely competent at managing her own domestic affairs when she had digs near Somerville and was an excellent hostess. She was very committed politically and did not get on particularly well with one or two fellows of her own college who were Socialists. Neither side in these circumstances seemed to make any attempt to understand the other. She was fairly rigid in her opinions. In terms of her own in-built beliefs and opinion she always knew exactly where she stood.

As Chairman of the Conservative Association he remembers that she worked hard to get interesting and unusual speakers. Quintin Hailsham, who was then the member for Oxford, was often called in to give support. She had already become a lively and amusing letter writer and would keep up long correspondences with friends on a regular basis. Whenever the Tories were asked to take part in a debate against Cambridge, or in canvassing or in village meetings, she was always game to come along and take part.

Perhaps because there were fewer of them, girls had to work extremely hard to keep up with the larger number of men proportionately in their finals. A girl at Oxford in that generation, therefore, however pretty she might be, had less chance of making a strong impression on the university as a whole. Margaret Roberts seems to be one of the few girls of her time whom a lot of people remember as being outstanding. She took a second in chemistry and a BSc, researching in crystallography, which was well up to standard, but it was in terms of her general ability that she really came to make an impact.

The end of her period at Oxford meant not only a break with Oxford itself, although in 1970 she was given the highest honour her college had to offer, an honorary fellowship of Somerville, but to some extent a break with Grantham too, since she now had to concentrate on earning her own living. Her links with her family, however, remained extremely close.

In 1952 Alfred Roberts, having been twenty-five years on the Council, an alderman for nine years, Mayor and chairman of the Finance Committee, was remarkably shabbily treated by Labour when they came to power there for the first time. Although he had been partly responsible for the election of the first Labour alderman, as a matter of fair play and because he thought that he was a good man personally, when Labour was the minority party, they now used their voting power ruthlessly. When he came to the first council meeting of the new civic year, together with the six other robed aldermen, he promptly found himself voted off in favour of a Socialist nominee. He quietly stood up, took off his robes and said, as reported by the *Grantham Journal*, so quietly that he could almost not be heard: 'No honours. No medals, only the satisfaction of knowing that a job has been well done. May God bless Grantham for ever.'

He left the council chamber and never went back to serve there again, although he could have if he had wanted to. He continued to play a leading part in the life of the borough in other ways, but he was obviously deeply hurt by what had happened for a very considerable time. It is hard to think of such a dedicated public servant being treated in this way.

He continued with his business until 1960 when he retired, sadly just before his wife's death. Beatrice Roberts had been ill for some time, after a major operation some five years previously, but she died quite suddenly. Later he remarried and his widow is still living at Grantham.

Alfred Roberts himself died on 10th February, 1970, at the age of 77, shortly after listening to his daughter broadcasting on the BBC. Although he did not live to see her become a member of the Cabinet later the same year, he had taken an immense satisfaction in her achievements.

He also had a fundamental effect on her career. In many ways he was the epitome of values which were the strength of provincial England. The qualities which he stood for, absolute probity, a determination to work for one's own family, a compassion for those less fortunate in the world and a belief that, far from the world owing one a living, one bore a responsibility to use one's opportunities for the general good, were ones which were to have a profound and lasting influence on his daughter's thinking.

3

'A Literate Type of Scientist'

The first thing Margaret Roberts had to do when she came down from Oxford was to find a job. The fact that she had got a second rather than a first effectively ruled out the prospect of an academic career but, in any case, she was already more interested in politics and in contact with political people than with academics. The idea of reading for the Bar, when she could afford to, was already at the back of her mind.

In the meantime BX (Plastics) at Manningtree, on the mouth of the River Stour in North East Essex, provided an ideal opportunity. It was a go-ahead firm with a staff of about seventy or eighty young graduates in its research laboratory, mostly concerned with various aspects of the development of plastics. Margaret Roberts was one of three girl graduates taken on there in September 1947. Stanley Booth, who was in charge of the research projects, can remember her starting there very well indeed. 'The young scientist with a second,' he says, 'is and always has been the real work-horse of the industry. What we were looking for was someone with a clear brain, a good practical training and his or her feet on the ground. Margaret Roberts fitted all these specifications perfectly.'

They were a hard-working, dedicated team, involved with all types of new plastic materials and their application. It was a deliberate policy, as Stanley Booth says, to look for people with practical minds who were willing to throw themselves into what they were doing and make an active contribution to the life of the establishment. Margaret Roberts fitted very well into this environment. She was not too much of a specialist, she could communicate well and she was more than prepared to take a trial product and go out and see how people got on with it in practice. In one particular case she spent some weeks working with a new product in the works of a jobbing printer and enjoyed herself enormously. Here, W. H. Dimsdale, who was a senior executive with BX, remembers her as a practical, friendly girl who was also a literate type of scientist. She was always keen to discuss things with people, whether it was the job in hand or politics.

Politics was known to be her principal interest. There are a number of people still in the Lawford, Manningtree and Mistley area who are members of the local Conservative Association (part of the Harwich Constituency) because she persuaded them to join in the first place. She was always prepared to talk about her views with anyone. Although there were a certain number of people at the laboratory with left-wing views at this particular period, and others who adopted a similar stance in order to tease her, it was all very good-hearted. W. E. Martin, another senior member of the staff, who is now retired and is living in Ipswich, recalls that he used to enjoy having political discussions with her. She was always very assured, despite her age, and could quote facts and figures with accuracy in support of her arguments. In her own work, he remembers, she was extremely methodical and he found her reports invariably methodical and clear. She was also very meticulous about her appearance. As things got easier with rationing there was a fair amount of entertaining going on among staff members from the laboratory and their wives, and it was a standing joke that Margaret Roberts would always go home and dress up properly before coming out to a party.

Joyce Duggan, who is now married and also living in Ipswich, was a member of the clerical staff and used to tease Margaret Roberts by saying, 'There goes the future prime minister.' She always took it in very good part and was very talkative and friendly, but Joyce Duggan remembers that she used to get so involved when arguing about politics that she would get very red with exertion. There seemed to be a sort of inner light about her, Joyce thought, which animated her entirely when she spoke. She was always rather proper and hated gossip.

Stanley Booth says that when she got on to a subject which she really knew well she almost visibly relaxed. She was quick to get to the root of a matter but she would never try and blind other people with irrelevant statistics as some politicians and particularly would-be politicians tend to do. She could be shy if she did not know the person she was talking to but was always ready to stick up for her opinions. Even at this stage he felt that she really wanted to make her career in politics, though she was a highly competent chemist.

While working at Manningtree, she had digs in Colchester and immediately joined the Colchester Young Conservatives, of which she became secretary of the town branch, and took part in other activities in the constituency. Philip Fell, who is now a solicitor practising in Suffolk, was then the branch chairman and he and his sister knew her well. He found her politically very well informed, clear-headed and immensely competent. She knew her speeches absolutely by heart before she made them and did not have to fall back on her notes. The constituency put her into a team for the national speaking competition which got as far as the finals of the Home Counties (North) Area. She generated tremendous enthusiasm about everything she did, but was always very professional where politics were concerned. Although she still can get very nervous before making a speech, even today, there was never any dither about her and she had a gift for simplifying an issue so that people could readily understand what she was talking about. It was a great time in the Conservative Party for re-thinking policies while they were in opposition largely under the influence of R. A. Butler. She was a particular enthusiast for Butler's Industrial Charter and took an informed and lively interest in the subject. Even at this stage, Philip Fell remembers, she had a predilection for hats.

Bill Jollife, who is now the Chairman of Colchester Conservative Association, was already an active member at this time. They had a young members group, bridging the gap between the YCs and the senior part of the Association and he persuaded her to become the secretary of this. He remembers how immensely hard she worked and also that there was a tremendous row because they had a service band from the Colchester Garrison at one of their dances and there were questions asked in the House about the Army taking part in a political function.

Among the people with whom she became friends through politics in Colchester was a Scottish farmer called Willie Cullen, who farmed at Ramsey near Harwich. She suggested that if he was driving back to Scotland on the Great North Road he might like to break the journey at Grantham and call in on her family. He did and met her sister Muriel and is now her brother-in-law.

The Cullens say that however dedicated she might be to politics she was always fun to have around. She was also capable of springing some surprises on them. Once, on a visit to Newmarket races, Margaret Roberts suddenly asked her sister what colour she thought her coat was. 'I don't know,' said Muriel Cullen, 'I should say it was Burnt Brown.' 'Good,' came the reply, 'I thought so too. There's a horse by that name in the next race and I've got a pound on it at ten to one.' It won.

She could also surprise them with the unexpected range of her knowledge. She had just got very interested in gardening and when staying with them asked about the names of the shrubs which they were growing. A few days later she had learnt them off by their Latin names as well.

The period which Margaret Roberts spent at Manningtree and Colchester gave her a good deal of political confidence. She had gained a lot of experience politically at Oxford and now she had had the opportunity of putting it to the test in practical circumstances. Lord Alport, who was then the candidate and later the Member of Parliament at Colchester, remembers how effective she was at meetings. Both he and his wife felt that she was someone quite out of the ordinary. She was beginning to feel herself that she was capable of taking on a constituency of her own.

It was as a representative from Colchester that Margaret Roberts went to the Conservative Party Conference at Llandudno in 1949. Among the delegates there was John Miller, the Chairman of the Dartford Constituency Association. During a break between the sessions he was talking to a friend who came from the Home Counties North area, which at that time included Colchester. Dartford was looking for a new candidate and he told his friend that they had no-one particular yet in mind. 'There's a girl called Margaret Roberts who's jolly good,' came the suggestion, 'and she's hoping to speak in today's debate. Why don't you come and listen to her?'

John Miller did hear her and was immediately impressed. When, a few weeks later, Dartford came round formally to selecting a candidate, Margaret Roberts was one of the people to whom he wrote. Once they had seen her there was never any question about whom they wanted to adopt.

One of the things that Margaret Roberts agreed with the Association was that she would come and live in the neighbourhood. She therefore had to give up her job at Manningtree and get one in the London area. For the next two years she worked in the central laboratories of J. Lyons and Company at Cadby Hall in Hammersmith, doing research into food and food technology. Once again she was a success in the job, being described as a thoughtful and careful researcher and very easy to get on with.

In order to travel from Dartford to Hammersmith and back each day she had to leave home at half-past six each morning and did not get get back until half-past six at night before doing a full evening's political work. She was lucky in finding a remarkably kind and friendly family with whom to live. Councillor Woollcott and his wife were both enthusiastic Conservatives and put a lot of energy into local activities and so they understood very well what she was trying to achieve. They were delighted to have her, both as a candidate and as a friend, and she became very much part of the family. The great thing, they both say, is how she seemed to enjoy everything so much. Mrs Woollcott in particular remembers a party which they gave for her own father's ninetieth birthday and the spontaneous pleasure which Margaret Roberts took in joining in the celebrations.

Dartford was certainly a tremendous challenge. An old borough on the south bank of the Thames about fifteen miles out of London, it also covered as a constituency a wide strip of northern Kent. It contained a mixture of mostly commuter housing and industry, including paper machinery and chemical and processed food manufacturing as well as the more traditional making of flour and beer. In 1950 the electorate stood at close on 80,000 which was large for the period. It had been represented in Parliament since the end of the war by Norman Dodds for Labour, a sincere and able member who was popular locally. As well as being a publicity and exhibition manager for the London branch of the Cooperative Wholesale Society he was an experienced political campaigner. Margaret Roberts was taking on one of the ablest people of his kind in the game and she knew it.

In fact they got on extremely well. As she was to prove in later elections, she never carried personalities into politics and was always extremely fastidious about the way in which she fought a campaign. As a result, although she fought well in both the elections of 1950 and 1951, she was well liked by the Socialists at Dartford as well as by her own people.

She worked extremely hard. When she got home, as soon as she had had a hot meal with the family, which Mrs Woollcott insisted on her taking, she would be out on a long programme of canvassing, meetings and other engagements, sometimes until quite late in the evening. She then had to be up again to leave for work early the following morning. It was at this stage in her life that she really developed her facility for getting by on only four or five hours sleep a night, which was to stand her in good stead later.

She was an indefatigable canvasser with a good memory for names and faces and she had the useful gift for a politician of usually being able to remember where she had met someone before. In spite of the rate at which she worked she never seemed to be worn out and she is described as having a capacity for getting her second wind rather sooner than most people can get their first. At this time, before redistribution, Dartford also included most of the present area of Erith and Crayford and there was a lot of territory to cover. Margaret Roberts would accept invitations to speak all over the constituency, at factory gates, at open-air meetings, at lunch-hour in the canteens, wherever the opportunity presented itself, and she could get there. She was invariably polite to her political opponents and this helped her to get the chance to put over her case. On one occasion she even inveigled the experienced Norman Dodds into taking part in a joint meeting with her at Dartford Grammar School, where to use the words of one of her enthusiastic supporters, 'She wiped the floor with him in the argument.' He never made the mistake of appearing with her on a joint platform again, though they did once appear together to dance an exhibition waltz in public at the Mayor's Charity Ball in Crayford to which each of them had been separately asked.

On formal occasions she was always beautifully turned out. Mrs Woollcott, who used sometimes to help her get ready, remembers the trouble she used to take about her clothes and her appearance and that she was an excellent needlewoman. They felt she was very modest about all her accomplishments, although she also kept up the piano while she was living with them.

At the general election of 1950 she scored 24,490 votes to Norman Dodds' 38,128, with a Liberal trailing at 5,011. It was not a bad result for the youngest woman candidate in the country particularly as she had only had a few months to nurse the seat. In the election of the following year, in a straight fight between Labour and Conservative, she cut the sitting member's majority by 1,300 and increased her own vote by more than 3,000. She also made a considerable impression nationally when she proposed the vote of thanks to Sir Winston Churchill at a mass rally of ten thousand women Conservatives in the Royal Albert Hall during 1950.

During 1951 she took a job for a short period as personal assistant to the director of the Joint Iron Council, a trade association of iron and steel users, in order to widen her industrial experience.

One of her proudest moments was when her father came to speak for her at Dartford, and Alfred Roberts in his turn was obviously undemonstratively but immensely proud of her. In 1961 when she ultimately succeeded Dame Pat Hornsby-Smith as Under-Secretary at the Ministry of Pensions his only comment was, 'I am absolutely delighted.'

She never seemed to be nonplussed by any mishaps which took place during election campaigns. Once, at one of her biggest meetings, all the lights went out and she waited quietly and without turning a hair while some of her supporters rushed to get candles so that she could get on with her speech.

Dartford was a happy and well-run Association and they were lucky in John Miller, a local builder, who was an excellent chairman. There was also a good deal of mutual aid from neighbouring constituencies in Kent and two of the other candidates fighting there at this time were Peter Kirk at Gravesend and Edward Heath at Bexley, who got in in 1950. Margaret Roberts also became friendly with Sir Alfred Bossom, the member for Maidstone, who was Chairman of the Kent Conservatives, and his family including Clive Bossom, who was later to serve as her first parliamentary private secretary in 1961.

In spite of a good candidate and an enthusiastic team, Dartford was never a real winner with the sort of built-in majority that Labour had there. Having fought there twice, she was certainly entitled to feel that she had served her political apprenticeship. In any event she had decided to get married.

Among her supporters in the Dartford campaigns was Major Denis Thatcher, the managing director of a family paint firm at Erith. Having served in the war in the Royal Artillery, in Sicily, Italy and France and gained a military MBE and two mentions in despatches, he had taken over the management of Atlas Preservative Company, who were chemical and paint manufacturers and marine degreasing engineers.

Luckily for the husband of a future prime minister, he met Margaret Roberts through politics. He got into the practice of driving her to meetings and, on polling-day, 1951, they announced their engagement.

They were married on 14th December, 1951 at Wesley's Chapel, one of the most famous of Methodist churches, in the City Road, London. The bride was dressed in a sapphire blue gown in velvet with a hat to match trimmed with dove grey ostrich feathers. She carried a matching muff. The wedding reception took place at the Bossom family's house at 5 Carlton Gardens where so many famous end-of-session parties were held for Conservative members in the years after the war. John Miller proposed the health of the bride and bridegroom and as a sign of how well liked they were in Dartford, Councillor Woollcott's ward, Heath Ward, alone gave them a solid silver tea service. They spent a honeymoon in Lisbon and Madeira and then went to live at Swan Court in Chelsea.

To all intents and purposes this was to mark a break in Margaret Thatcher's political life of nearly seven years. During this time she was to produce a family, be called to the Bar and build up a practice of her own as a barrister. But she was not to find a constituency that could give her entry into the House of Commons until 1958. Even then, when she did, she was only thirty-three.

4

Twins – and a Call to the Bar

From the end of 1951 onwards Margaret Thatcher was very much occupied with being a housewife. She had time to revive a number of old hobbies like music and cooking and develop newer ones like gardening. In 1953 she had twins, a boy and a girl called Mark and Carol, who are now twenty-two and qualified respectively as a chartered accountant and a solicitor. She has always been very good at separating her family from the kind of publicity that makes life burdensome for a politician's close relations and she concentrated her life increasingly on her husband and the children. Denis Thatcher was in the meantime becoming an increasingly influential figure in industry and had become director of a number of companies until eventually, as a director of Burmah Oil Trading Ltd, he found himself doing the reverse of commuting and driving down each day from London to Swindon and back. The rest of their time they spent between a house in Chelsea and a home in Kent, though they also found time to enjoy ski-ing, tennis and the theatre.

In the meanwhile she had found enough to keep her mind extremely busy. In 1950, while she was still nursing Dartford and working at Lyons, she had joined Lincoln's Inn as a student. In 1954, only a few months after the birth of the twins, she was called to the Bar. It was the culmination of an ambition which she had had for a very long time but it also gave her the opportunity to combine her very considerable mental powers with bringing up a family.

As a scientist there might have been an obvious temptation to opt for the

51

Patent Bar, which specialises in technical scientific matters and is an extremely lucrative form of practice, if rather cut off from the legal mainstream. She chose instead to throw herself in at the deep end of her profession. She started by doing a common law pupillage at the now Lord Justice Lawton's chambers in the Temple at 5 King's Bench Walk. They were a well-known set of chambers with a wide variety of common law cases and criminal matters, presided over by one of the best-known clerks of his day, the late Stanley Hopkins. Even the senior members of the Bar were all said to stand in awe of him and most of them certainly did. Stanley (clerks in barristers' chambers are invariably known by their Christian names rather than their surnames) was in a position to provide a pupil with a great deal of experience at magistrates' courts, county courts, inquests and the like. This experience of advocacy was to stand her in good stead later in Parliamentary debates. One of the junior tenants at 5 King's Bench Walk at this time was Airey Neave, already the member for Abingdon, whom she had known from her days in the candidates association. He was later to play a leading part in supporting her election as leader of the Conservative Party.

After having finished the first part of her pupillage she went, on the advice of Sir John Senter, a well-known commercial lawyer, to do a six-month specialised pupillage with Peter Rowland, a tax expert in chambers next door at 6 King's Bench Walk. She had chosen this particular form of training, he remembers, rather than the Patent Bar because she was determined to go into politics and wanted as wide a field of experience as possible, particularly in matters of financial legislation.

From there she went, as a tenant, into the chambers of B. M. J. Bonner, a well-established chancery practitioner at 5 New Square, Lincoln's Inn. As far as the Chancery Bar was concerned it was a mixed set since it contained some members who practised regularly as advocates in that division like the late Michael Stranders, QC and a number of others who did only tax and advisory work. As in other stages of her career members of her chambers remember her as working extremely hard, having a very clear and concise brain and being remarkably well coordinated as far as running her practice as well as a home was concerned.

Although Margaret Thatcher only practised for five years as a barrister the experience was obviously important to her. It brought her into contact with a wide selection of legal matters. It gave her the opportunity of getting used to presenting a case quickly from an already prepared brief. And above all it underlined to her how important the effects of carefully drafted legislation were where this was going to impinge on people's everyday lives and how dangerous or oppressive could be the results of unnecessary or badly drawn-up Acts of Parliament.

5

'She's in a Class of Her Own. . .'

In 1958 her political luck finally changed. She had kept her hand in by speaking for the Central Office and taking part in the Conservative Candidates Association meetings, but although she was interviewed and short-listed by a number of constituencies the answer had regularly been the same. Selection committees were impressed by her, they liked her but they simply were not sure enough about having a young mother with two small children as their member. Having won her spurs at Dartford she did not want to go back to fighting a hopeless or a marginal seat. Leading Conservatives who had been impressed with her work there and at candidates' conferences strongly advised her to look for a winnable seat next time she stood. Although she had more potential than many of the candidates who did take part in the 1955 election she did not find a seat to fight. Oblivious of the fact that she was able to combine a taxing professional life with looking after her family, constituency associations seemed determined to go on thinking of her as a housewife. It was, until fairly recently, a continual dilemma for young and able women in British politics.

Fortunately not all constituencies thought like this. At the beginning of 1958 it became likely that a general election would not be too far postponed (it was held eventually in the autumn of the following year). A number of older members who wanted to retire began to give their associations warning so that they could adopt new candidates. Among these was Finchley, where the sitting member, Sir John Crowder, had been installed since 1935. Sir John was an Etonian with a long period of service on the Hampshire County Council as well as in Parliament and he had held a number of offices on the 1922 Committee. He was the father of Peter Crowder, QC, the present member for Ruislip–Northwood.

In the general pattern of things, constituencies often go for a change when they have to choose a new candidate after an existing member, however popular, has sat there for a long time. An association that has had a minister representing the seat very often choses someone they think will be likely to be an active backbencher; one that has had an establishment figure will select someone younger and less set in his ways. Sir John was essentially one of a number of senior Tory backbenchers whom the press termed 'Knights of the Shire' and her contrast to him proved to be Margaret Thatcher's chance. She made a sufficiently strong impression at the selection committee to be picked by a comfortable margin. So began an extremely happy relationship with Finchley which has lasted to this day.

The Borough of Finchley, as the seat was then called (it was an amalgam of Finchley itself and part of the Friern Barnet Urban District Council at this period, but has now been reconstituted as part of the London Borough of Barnet) was an interesting constituency in many ways. It covered an area stretching over a considerable length of the Barnet line and included no less than five major commuting underground stations: East, Central and West Finchley, Woodside Park and Totteridge and Whetstone. Most of the houses were owner-occupied, in places like Totteridge and Hampstead Garden Suburb, but there was also a certain amount of industry and quite large sectors of council housing. It was a fair barometer of intelligent public feeling since the electors there did not hesitate to express their views on national as well as parochial matters.

This was one of the places that the Liberal Party was to pin their hopes on in the early 1960s, planning to make it a bridgehead in the North London suburbs as they did with Orpington in South London. They put up a number of their most promising candidates here, including Manuella Sykes in 1955 and John Pardoe, now the member for North Cornwall, in 1964. In 1955 Sir John Crowder's majority had been 12,925. With a slightly smaller electorate, Margaret Thatcher raised this to 16,260 in 1959. The Socialist candidate on this occasion was Eric Deakins, currently a minister in the present Labour government.

She worked in Finchley just as she had at Dartford, meeting people, talking to them, getting to know them, listening to their views. Ray Langston, who has been her agent for thirteen years, describes her as an exceptionally good constituency member. 'When I first went to Finchley in 1962,' he says, 'I was a little bit nervous about how I would get on, working with a woman member. I need not have worried. She comes to the constituency regularly. She holds special surgeries whenever they are required. Irrespective of what job she is doing in

Parliament she works hard for the interests of her constituents. She is always available to people, whether they are her political supporters or not. She is always keen on going round the division and seeing things for herself at first hand so that she can make up her own mind about them. She does know individuals and their personal problems. How she does it all heaven only knows.'

Over the years Margaret Thatcher has built up her personal following in Finchley to a very high degree. She works well with people of all kinds and has taken a regular part in local life. She knows a great many people there by name which is always one of the marks of a good constituency MP. She has got the reputation for being very much on the ball with constituency matters, answering letters promptly and taking pains with them. 'You feel,' one constituent puts it, 'that she really does represent the whole place and she is always good at keeping in touch.' The fact that she is well respected locally has stood her in good stead in difficult years, like 1964, when the Liberals made their major onslaught, and 1974 when, as a result of boundary changes, she lost 19,000 of her electors and several of her best Conservative wards to neighbouring constituencies.

There is a good account of her campaign organisation in David Butler's book *The British General Election of 1964* (Macmillan), where Finchley was one of the constituencies picked out for detailed analysis. In this book she is described, after only five years in Parliament, as a formidable sitting member, who maintained good relations with the various groups in the Finchley constituency, including the trade unions. Margaret Thatcher's capacity for getting on well with people, whether they agreed with her politically or not, and listening to their points of view is an important personal asset. A fractious or small-minded opponent, who sees an election in terms of personal animosities, can make a campaign an unpleasant experience for everybody. Margaret Thatcher always fights in terms of political issues and though she can hit hard in argument relies on persuasion and not gimmicks or animosity. Her father's influence here is very clear.

Her other great strength lies in organisation itself. The Association works as a team, everybody knows what their job is, nothing is left to chance. Organisation has traditionally been one of the great Conservative strengths though in recent years this has been under some strain in terms of national politics. A leader who is aware of the importance of not only having the right policies but being able to put them over can be an important factor as far as the party is concerned.

When she entered the House of Commons in October 1959, although she was known to a number of members personally and through the candidates association, she was still a comparatively unknown quantity. Sir Alfred Bossom had advised her to broaden the basis of her political knowledge as much as possible and this she had done, but at Westminster she still remained serious-minded and rather shy. John Marling, the Conservative Whip's Chief Clerk, who is an experienced and extremely well-liked figure at the House, has seen generations of Members of Parliament come and go. When Margaret Thatcher was first adopted at Finchley, he can remember Sir John Crowder saying to him, 'Greatly as I deplore it, my successor is going to be a woman, but she is very able.' He was interested to see what she would turn out to be like. When she arrived at Westminster he was very impressed.

Despite their difficulty in getting into the House, it was an era of able female members on the Conservative side. They included Eveline Hill, who sat for Manchester (Wythenshawe), Edith Pitt, the member for Birmingham (Edgbaston), Evelyn Emmet, the member for East Grinstead, Pat Hornsby-Smith for Chislehurst, Joan Vickers for Plymouth (Devonport), Mervyn Pike for Melton and the proverbial Dame Irene Ward. Margaret Thatcher quickly learned to hold her own in this distinguished company.

John Marling can recollect a number of things standing out about her at this particular time. She was obviously politically gifted but she made it clear to him that her family came first as far as her career was concerned. She made a practice of beginning the day with the children at her then home at Farnborough in Kent and would always give them breakfast, get them ready for school and drop them off at the school gates herself before going to the House. She was inclined to stand in the background before she was really certain of herself but she learned to find her way quickly. She did not speak often but when she did it was listened to because she spoke with accuracy and authority. She obviously took trouble to do her homework. With some people, as he puts it, it is the same old music all the time but when Margaret Thatcher came out with something it was well prepared and well thought out. She never over-stretched herself and always remained calm and cool, both in committee and in the House itself.

The Tory Party, as John Marling says, is run by loyalty and not by discipline. Although she was more than capable of standing up to the Whips on a matter of principle, she was not one of those members who always put herself first, she did not have to be chased the whole time to get her into the division lobby and she never left the House unless she had registered a pair, a cardinal virtue for the Whips' organisation.

Her regular pair from 1959 until he retired in 1974 was Charles Pannell, the Labour member for Leeds (West), now Lord Pannell. He can remember her from the time that she was fighting Norman Dodds at Dartford, since he himself had been Mayor of Erith and had long links with Kent. Charles Pannell, who became a senior Labour minister, was also an extremely experienced Parliamentary hand

and a great upholder of the House and its traditions. He had an agreeable professional relationship with her and found her easy to get on with. She never broke a pair or went back on an agreement once it had been made. She was also a great believer in Parliament itself. He can remember her expressing her admiration for the late Bessie Braddock, one of the best constituency members the House has ever seen. 'That's the one,' she said to him. 'She's in a class of her own as a member.'

Each new session of Parliament produces a fresh ballot for private members bills. In the ballot of November 1959 Margaret Thatcher drew third place, the only woman member to draw one on this occasion. This must have put her in something of a quandary. She was inexperienced as to the ways of the House and even as to the details of its procedure and had not even made her maiden speech. Now she had the chance of piloting through a piece of legislation which might well reach the statute book (the first three bills drawn usually stand a good chance of doing so unless they are too highly contentious).

She originally wanted to introduce a bill tidying up the law on contempt of court but Sir Reginald Manningham-Buller (now Lord Dilhorne), who was then Attorney-General, took the view that this was too complicated a task for a backbench member who was not even a silk at the time. After a vigorous argument with the Whips, in which neither she nor Martin Redmayne minced words, she decided instead to introduce the Public Bodies (Admission of the Press to Meetings) Bill.

This arose out of a major controversy which had been generated during the printing dispute the previous summer when a number of Labour-controlled councils had refused to admit reporters to their meetings if the papers for which they worked had been declared 'black' by the unions. Many people disagreed strongly with this on the basis that the first duty of local councils was to the public who had elected them and that the public had a right to know about what their representatives were doing. As *The Times* put it in a leading article at the time of the Bill, this involved 'a great constitutional principle' which sought to vindicate 'the liberty of the subject to be fully informed of public affairs and read independent comment on them.'

When the Bill was published it was sponsored, as well as by Margaret Thatcher by, among others, Sir Lionel Heald, an ex-Attorney General, Captain (now Sir) Fred Corfield, Peter Kirk, Sir Robert Grimston and Wing Commander Robert Grant-Ferris, later the Chairman of Ways and Means and Deputy-Speaker. The title specified that it would provide 'for the admission of representatives of the press to the meetings of certain bodies exercising public functions.' Here Margaret Thatcher and her fellow sponsors ran into procedural difficulties

almost at once. The point was raised by a number of members on the Second
Reading debate that the principle involved should be extended to give a statutory
right to the public as well to be admitted to full meetings of local councils. The
original title had specified admission for the press. A small but active group of
Labour members began to use the rules of procedure to halt the progress of the
Bill. A government motion was rquired to make provision for members of the
public to be brought within its scope and this Henry Brooke, the Minister for
Housing and Local Government, promptly set down. Gerry Reynolds, the
Labour Member for North Islington, got in first by tabling a motion to introduce
an entirely new Bill, with the same title, under the ten-minute rule procedure,
which would be debated later. When Margaret Thatcher attempted to replace
'press' by 'public' in the text of her Bill by an amendment, there was an objection
by him on a point of order. 'On a question of fact,' the Speaker ruled, 'the
honourable gentleman is quite right. His motion beat the other one by forty
minutes.'

After a rather unedifying struggle in which an attempt was made by opposition
members to amend the Bill to limit its provision to circumstances where there
was 'no interruption in the normal production of newspapers and periodicals', a
further motion to bring the whole procedure under a standardised 'code of
conduct' was defeated in committee. There was a good deal of negotiation behind
the scenes and finally Gerry Reynolds and his friends bowed to the inevitable,
providing certain alterations were made to the text of the Bill by agreement
during the committee stage. The County Councils Association were also concerned lest legislation should break too deeply into what they regarded as the
necessarily confidential character of some of their proceedings, disclosure of
which, they felt, would be against the public interest. Margaret Thatcher equally
was determined that neither the press nor the public should be excluded by a
council going into committee on one of their main meetings in order to avoid
publicity.

In the end the committee stage got through by the end of April 1964 and the
Bill was then ready to be sent to the Lords. As *The Times* ruefully pointed out, it
in fact emerged with a somewhat different look. Committee meetings exercising
delegated functions of main authorities were excluded from its scope, but three
basic principles remained unscathed. Both the press and the public were to be
admitted to main meetings of a whole Council as of right. The number of
legitimate grounds for excluding the press on a temporary basis under Arthur
Henderson's earlier Act of 1908 were strictly limited. And the device of
excluding anybody by a council resolving itself into committee was effectively
blocked.

At the Third Reading on 14th May, 1970, she accepted two further minor amendments, providing that at council meetings the members could accept advice from their officers in private, and conferring privilege, so far as actions for defamation were concerned, on authorities and their officers with regard to matter contained in any document supplied by them to the press as part of such a meeting.

In the House of Lords the Bill was moved by Lady Elliot of Harewood. It was the first time that a woman had sponsored legislation in the upper house and the first Act of Parliament taken right through both houses by women members. It received the Royal Assent in October 1960 and took effect as from 1st June of the following year.

It was a major achievement for an inexperienced member and the way that Margaret Thatcher handled the proceedings drew her a great deal of praise from many quarters. She took the almost unprecedented step of making her maiden speech in introducing her own Bill on 5th February rather than breaking herself in gently on some easier matter. It is normal on these occasions for a new member to make a formal introduction of him or herself to the House by speaking about his own constituency and his predecessors in it. Margaret Thatcher was determined to get her Bill through and not to waste time. 'This is a maiden speech,' she said, 'but I know that the constituency of Finchley which I have the honour to represent would not wish me to do other than come straight to the point and address myself to this matter.' And come to the point she did, hardly even referring to the notes which she had made.

Fred Corfield, in seconding the Bill, made the point that it was not often that anybody had the opportunity of both congratulating a maiden speaker and congratulating at the same time a member who was introducing a by-no-means unimportant piece of legislation 'in a manner which would do credit to the Front Bench on either side of the Chamber.'

Henry Brooke, in summing up for the government, spoke with similar enthusiasm: 'She spoke with charm, she spoke with a fluency which most of us would envy and she achieved the rare feat of making a Parliamentary reputation on a Friday (the day which is normally reserved for private member's business), a reputation which I am sure she will now proceed to enhance, on the earlier days of the week.'

Opposition speakers were equally generous. Michael Stewart, from the Front Bench, described her speech as a most 'striking, impressive and skilful performance'. Barbara Castle spoke of an outstanding maiden speech. And Charles Pannell, her pair, said that it was 'rather a beautiful maiden speech' but could not resist the typical dig that perhaps it could also be a model to the occupants of the

Government Front Bench 'on how to deliver a speech in favour of a Bill, instead of having a dreary essay read to us in a turgid monotone'.

The House is usually kindly to maiden speakers but this reaction went well beyond the normal run. As Sir Keith Joseph put it later, speaking as Parliamentary Secretary to the Ministry of Housing and Local Government, on the Third Reading of the Bill, 'This has proved a delicate and contentious measure, perhaps not ideally suited to a first venture into legislation, but the House will remember from all stages of the Bill the cogent, charming, lucid and composed manner of my honourable friend.'

The impression which she made in presenting the Bill certainly had an immediate impact on her further career. But although she was well thought of in official circles, she was still not necessarily always prepared to toe the line. She was one of a group of Conservative MPs who defied the Whips later in the year in voting on the Criminal Justice Bill, by backing a clause to restore corporal punishment for young offenders on a second or subsequent conviction for crimes of violence. She also maintained an independent stand when discussing a number of matters in party committees.

In the autumn of 1972 Dame Pat Hornsby-Smith who was the Joint Parliamentary Secretary to the Ministry of Pensions and National Insurance resigned to take up an opening in Commerce, which she badly wanted to accept. Margaret Thatcher's name was put forward for the job and Harold Macmillan, who was the Prime Minister, approved; but first he telegrammed the Minister concerned, John Boyd-Carpenter (now Lord Boyd-Carpenter), who was in Canada at the time for his agreement. 'Delighted,' came back the signal and Denis Thatcher, who was on a business journey to Japan, first heard of the appointment on the BBC news.

Margaret Thatcher's own comment was characteristic: 'We have three out of a present total of thirteen Conservative women now holding government jobs,' she said, 'which isn't a bad proportion, but I would like to see more women MPs.'

At the Ministry of Pensions she shared her functions with Richard Sharples, who was later tragically murdered as Governor of Bermuda. She was concerned with National Insurance matters and Supplementary Benefits, he with War Pensions and Industrial Injuries. Lord Boyd-Carpenter recalls a certain hesitation about the appointment of a young woman with two children to the job on the part of the permanent Secretary, Sir Eric Bowyer, and the other senior civil servants. 'She would turn up looking as if she had spent the whole morning with the coiffeur and the whole afternoon with the couturier. But we got at least as much work from her as from anyone else and probably a bit more. She was an absolutely full-time minister and they all became devoted to her.'

The only thing that civil servants in the department did not become so devoted to was her habit in an enormous number of cases of sending back letters which they had prepared dealing with constituency problems to be rewritten in her own terms. It was a practice which she shared in common with her then immediate chief and one which she has continued to do even as a senior minister herself.

A great deal of the work she was involved with, particularly with regard to National Insurance matters, was extremely complex and here she had the facility of picking up a brief both quickly and competently. She took a good deal of the department's legislation through the House, where her training as a lawyer certainly helped her, since much of it was legal in character. She was, Lord Boyd-Carpenter says, extremely good in the House both with questions and in debate. 'The only trouble was,' he comments, 'that when she really got going on an argument you had to almost pull her off the opposition Front Bench when she started to chase them about. The Chief Whip used to tell me to hurry her on with the legislation in hand. I think she thought it was a little bit unsporting when I did because she was enjoying herself so much.'

After John Boyd-Carpenter was transferred to the Treasury as Chief Secretary in July 1962, Margaret Thatcher stayed on at the Ministry of Pensions as junior minister to Niall Macpherson (now Lord Drumalbyn) with whom she also had a very good working relationship. Her then PPS, Sir Clive Bossom, the former member for Leominster, sums up her career at this point: 'After about four months in the job, she knew the National Insurance and Benefit rates as well as any civil servant in her office. She may have been a bit tactless in the beginning but she learnt extremely fast. As a minister, you knew exactly where you were with her. She was a breath of fresh air.' Above all, what she valued about the Ministry of Pensions at this point was that it was a ministry concerned with people, where she could make the results of her work as human as possible. She proved herself readily receptive to new ideas if they would help the people for whom she was responsible. She liked the Ministry and she stayed there until the Conservative Government fell in 1964.

6

People are More Important than Politics

The Conservatives were to be in opposition for nearly six years. During this time Margaret Thatcher held a wide range of shadow Front Bench appointments. By the end of it she had established a claim to be considered as an almost automatic choice for membership of the Shadow Cabinet and one of the leading Conservative speakers in the House.

It is interesting to look at the list of Front Bench appointments which she held, because not only does it show the increasing part she played between 1964 and 1970 in the counsels of her own party but it belies the suggestion that has sometimes been made that she is short on Front Bench experience.

When the party first went into opposition in October 1964, she continued in the field of pensions and national insurance as a junior spokesman. In October the following year she was transferred to a similar responsibility with housing and land. She stayed there until March 1966, when she became a junior Front Bench spokesman in Treasury matters. In October 1967, she was made a member of the Shadow Cabinet and became chief opposition spokesman on power. In October 1968, she took on the same responsibility with regard to transport, finally becoming, in October 1969, the shadow minister of education.

In addition, in the period in opposition during 1974, she was shadow minister for the environment and had further experience on financial matters.

The gap in this list is obviously foreign affairs and defence, and Labour spokesmen have made a great deal of this. When she was asked about foreign affairs and defence after her election as leader she was quoted by *Time* magazine as merely saying, 'I am all for them', but there is an apparent flippancy about this remark which seems to be out of keeping with her real concern, as shown by her more recent speeches concerned with world affairs and the maintenance of the Atlantic Alliance in the cause of world peace. What is by no means certain is whether or not having held a senior position in these particular fields is anything like the disadvantage that it might have proved even twenty years ago. Important as they are, the British people's primary problem at this stage is to meet the menace of inflation and here Margaret Thatcher's previous experience has admirably suited her for the major task.

In her first shadow job she was on familiar ground at pensions. But she was still determined to break new ground even though the party was in opposition and was engaged in fighting the Wilson government regularly in the House of Commons. One of the most significant features that arose from this period of her time in opposition was the fact that she began to work with Airey Neave and some other Conservative members to achieve pensions for the over-eighties, a belated act of justice which was finally honoured when the party came to power in 1970.

After she left the specific field of pensions, however, in 1965, she began a process of continually broadening her range. Of all the roles which she played in opposition perhaps the one which she enjoyed most in the House of Commons was finance. But the activities of the first two Wilson governments gave a good deal of scope to those who were responsible for opposing them in the House. In criticising government ministers, in whatever sector she was involved with, her speeches were always extremely accurate and extremely well-prepared. As a lawyer, as she once said herself in the House, she liked to be able to acknowledge her authorities when she cited them.

As a chemist, she has always been good at handling complex structures. There is a sense of order and balance about her speeches as a shadow spokesman which still makes them impressive reading although many of the issues with which they were involved have changed. But it is interesting also to see how often she returned in opposition to the same subjects which were the keystone of her political philosophy. It was with the position of the individual in a constantly more and more bureaucratic world that she was consistently concerned: at housing with the struggle against a potentially overpowering Land Commission and to maintain the rights of the local ratepayer, at transport to safeguard the position of the commuter, a vast number of whom were involved with the increasing problems of British Rail and London Transport, at education to preserve the principle of parental choice.

During the 1965–66 period she was also much involved with the problems of the individual on a constituency basis, since Gerald Brooke, the English lecturer who was arrested and imprisoned in Russia on a highly oppressive charge, was one of her constituents at Finchley and she played a prominent part in the campaign to secure his release. Interestingly enough, the USSR was one of the countries which she visited on fact-finding tours while in opposition.

During this period she became a highly regarded speaker at the party conference and at meetings in various parts of the country as well as in the House. She was developing into a very poised and effective speaker and at the 1970 election was one of the comparatively few leading speakers on either side who could command sizeable audiences. But, despite the poise, she was still capable of being deeply moved herself as she showed in her speech, as Shadow Minister of Power, on the Aberfan inquiry. Much of it was a highly detailed survey of the evidence concerned but, in what she described as perhaps the most difficult and tragic debate in which she had ever taken part, she also said: 'There is a far greater bond in this disaster than any party political affiliation could indicate. All of us who are here have felt with the people of Aberfan that day. It would be disastrous enough to lose a child—I think it is the greatest disaster that can befall any family—but to lose a child in that way was so terrible that words can hardly express how we felt.' The whole House, she added, spoke as ordinary men and women in that regard. Nothing that they could do for the people of Aberfan could be too much. There are occasions when the House can speak with almost one voice. Like many of the speakers that day from both sides of the chamber, Margaret Thatcher was expressing the feeling that, in the long run, people are more important than politics. It is a principle which she is never likely to forget.

Margaret Roberts, aged four *(left)* with her sister Muriel

Above Margaret Roberts *(right)* with her parents and sister Muriel during her father's year as Mayor of Grantham

Above At the age of 21, after coming down from Oxford

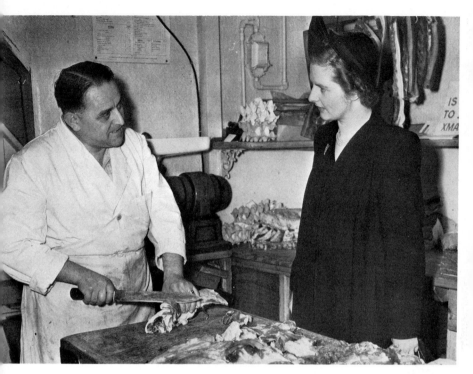

Above Margaret Roberts canvassing in Dartford during her unsuccessful campaign in 1951

Above Canvassing in Dartford

Above Margaret Thatcher with Dr Charles Hill *(left)* and Dame Patricia Hornsby-Smith *(right)*

Above Margaret Roberts at a Buckingham Palace Garden Party

Denis Thatcher with Margaret Roberts

Above A wedding-day portrait of Margar
Thatcher with her husband, Denis Tha
cher

Left Mrs Thatcher with her twin childr
Mark and Carol, in 1953

above The new MP for Finchley, Margaret Thatcher arrives at the House of Commons after her election in 1959

right Margaret Thatcher ski-ing in Tganri, 1962

Above The Government Fro
Bench at the State Opening
Parliament in July 1970. *Fro
left,* Francis Pym, Sir A
Douglas-Home, Reginald Mau
ling, Edward Heath, Ian Macle
Sir Keith Joseph, Geoffrey R
pon and Margaret Thatcher

Left 1970. The only woman
the Cabinet, Margaret Th
cher, Minister of Educati
talks to Edward Heath *(left)* a
Quintin Hogg

7

On the Side of the Angels

At the general election which took place on 18th June, 1970, Edward Heath was returned with a majority of thirty over all the other parties. The result was a triumph for the Tories and a contradiction of the way which most of the opinion polls had been going during the campaign, where by the end of the second week the National Opinion Poll in particular had shown the Socialists as much as 12·4% ahead. It was also a notable success for the Conservative leader who had never wavered in his presentation of the issues even when things seemed to be going against him. Labour appeared discredited with the electors on account of their failure to implement trade union reform and to come to grips with economic problems. Harold Wilson's personal campaign to turn the election into a presidential-style walkabout in the middle of a euphoric summer came particularly unstuck with a public which preferred watching the World Cup on television. George Brown, Labour's number two, who had also campaigned vigorously up and down the country, even lost his own seat at Belper.

At Finchley Margaret Thatcher increased her majority to 11,185, giving her 25,480 votes to her Labour opponent's 14,295, with the Liberal trailing at 7,614 a swing of 2,890 in her favour. With her previous experience in government and her service as a shadow minister, she was certain to get high office and when the cabinet was announced on 20th June she was made Secretary of State for Education and Science. She was also appointed a Privy Councillor.

This was a job which she was to hold for three and a half years during the whole period of the Heath Government. Although it was a position which had been held with distinction by another Conservative post-war minister, Dame Florence Horsburgh, as well as by Ellen Wilkinson on the other side, it was by no means an easy one. In the first place there was a particularly unfair assumption by

65

some political commentators that every cabinet had to have its statutory woman and that she had been slotted into this particular post for this purpose. Secondly, women ministers were not particularly well thought of by the public at that time because of Barbara Castle's disastrous climb-down to her colleagues over her proposed trade union legislation. Thirdly, it was a big spending department which was bound to bring her into argument, if not into conflict, with her own colleagues in the Treasury.

There were also a range of problems within the educational world itself. Twenty-five years had gone by since the passing of R. A. Butler's fundamental Education Act of 1944 and there was general agreement that the time had now come for new and major developments. There was strong controversy, however, among politicians, educationalists and the public as to what form these developments should take. A slow record of economic growth, particularly over the last decade, also meant that there was only a limited amount of money available to implement decisions when they were made.

Action was necessary on a number of matters which were still in the pipeline arising out of the reports of committees appointed by a previous Conservative government, including those chaired by Sir John Newsom on Primary Schools, Lord Robbins on Higher Education and Lady Plowden on Nursery Schools. There was the difficult financial problem of completing the Butler system by implementing Parliament's decision to raise the school leaving age to sixteen. There was a new responsibility for the department with regard to the education of mentally handicapped children under the recently passed Education (Handicapped Children) Act of 1970. Above all, there was the vexed and highly emotive question of comprehensive education, which had political as well as economic implications of considerable importance.

Under the Labour government there had been a major switch from the principle of leaving decisions on secondary education in the hands of the elected local authorities to imposing a uniform comprehensive solution throughout the country, regardless of circumstances and resources. As Secretary for Education, Anthony Crosland had issued two directives, Circular 10/65, which required local councils to produce their comprehensive plans for the minister's approval, and Circular 10/66, which used the building programme as a sanction against those who did not toe the line.

The Conservatives had made it clear over the years and in their 1970 manifesto that such an inflexible solution was unacceptable. As Margaret Thatcher herself was to put it in the first big debate on education in the new Parliament: 'A rigid system is the enemy of advance.' Without opposing changes of policy from the system of selection at 11+ where these were most suitable to the needs of the local community, as she showed by approving the comprehensive scheme submitted by heads shortly after her appointment, she underlined that the main criterion was the needs of the children concerned. As she told Parliament: 'In some ways the debate about the type of schools has perhaps distracted attention away from what is every bit as important, namely, what happens inside the schools.'

Accordingly she issued her own circular, known as 10/70, which made her own aims very clear. All children should be given full opportunities for secondary education suitable to their needs and abilities. A uniform pattern was rejected, as were restrictions on the character of secondary school building. Local authorities were to be free to determine the character of what they would provide in their own areas, subject to consultation with teachers and parents and to the schemes which they put forward providing full educational opportunity, being cost-effective and fulfilling local needs and wishes. As the minister put it: 'Where there is so much to be done for schools in deprived and poor areas, it seems to me to be a misuse of resources and effort to concentrate on upsetting a scheme which is working well when we should be trying to help those where opportunity is less than equal.'

An unfortunate problem at the beginning of her period at the department proved to be relations with the press. Shortly after her appointment as shadow minister the previous autumn there had been a difficult session at a lunch with the educational correspondents at the Cumberland Hotel at which she was the principal speaker, where there had been a good deal of frank, not to say rancorous, speaking on education topics. As Bruce Campbell, the extremely experienced correspondent of the *Daily Express*, puts it, even journalists who worked for normally Conservative newspapers were tearing their hair out and Margaret Thatcher seemed to have made her mind up that everybody there were mostly left-wing propagandists. What was being expressed was largely an in-built sense of geographical injustice but it was widely felt that she had reacted to these views with the feeling that the majority of correspondents was hostile or biased in favour of Socialist theories in education.

This was particularly to be regretted since Margaret Thatcher was probably more receptive to ideas than a good many of her predecessors but her relationship with Fleet Street certainly seemed to have got off to a bad start. It is probably true to say that she came into office with a certain amount of prejudice against her on the part of the press and a sticky press conference after she had been in the job for only a few days did not exactly help things. However, as time went on and her work became increasingly well documented, she got a steadily better press over the period she was in office. The more it was seen that she was prepared to fight, and fight hard, for more nursery schools, for replacing sub-standard primary schools and for a genuine maintenance of academic standards and expansion of education the more the majority of educational correspondents began to feel that she was a good minister. As one senior correspondent put it: 'Although she may have been a bit tactless to start with, she was certainly a lady on the side of the angels.'

The position with the press and the media was important because, from early on in the Heath Government, Margaret Thatcher was deputed to carry through two of its most controversial pieces of legislation, the abolition of free milk for older children in the schools and the introduction of entry charges into national museums and galleries. Both were fund-raising exercises to enable the government to raise money for what it regarded as more important calls on the revenue but each in a different way caused a storm of protest.

The argument over school milk became a highly complicated one ranging over a variety of subjects of a social, medical and nutritional character. Arguments and statistics against were extensively canvassed both in Parliament and the press and the Minister was dubbed, on account of her part in the proposals, 'Margaret Thatcher, milk-snatcher', a nickname which was to stick to her for most of the rest of her time in that office. Museum charges was a more peripheral responsibility since, in a sense, this measure came under the Minister for the Arts, the Paymaster-General, Viscount Eccles. But since the latter was in the Lords and his department came under the general umbrella of the Department of Education and Science, the latter were responsible for taking the enabling legislation through the House of Commons.

The actual amount of money produced by both schemes was in fact quite small in overall terms, less than £5 million a year, but the political damage which they did the Conservative Government with highly articulate sections of the community was out of all proportion. Although Margaret Thatcher was keenly sensitive to the need to save money, particularly since her own department needed to ask for increased estimates to maintain and improve on the basic educational programme, she became personally more sceptical about the actual advantage of either. Nevertheless they were Government policies for which the Cabinet as a whole was collectively in favour and acting on her principle of never asking someone else (ie one of her junior ministers) to do what she was not willing to undertake herself, she took a leading part in the debates involved.

Both measures were eventually carried, though the museum charges provisions were modified to allow the money raised to remain with the museums and galleries, largely as a result of a brilliant campaign organised by Hugh Leggatt and other leading figures in the art world. This scheme was eventually rescinded when Labour came to power, but it is interesting that, despite their vehement opposition at the time, the Socialists have made no attempt to reintroduce universal free milk in schools, and have themselves increased the charges for school meals and have admitted that there were no overriding medical factors involved.

If real steps forward were to be made in education, money was needed and there was a real requirement for frugal housekeeping in the department wherever this was possible. From 1970 onwards Margaret Thatcher made it clear, in her speeches and her management of her own department, that she was strongly aware that the chief thing that mattered was the control of inflation. As her White Paper on Education in 1972 showed, there was a need for an increase in expenditure, but only against the general framework of proper checks and balances being applied. If, as a nation, we were going to spend more money it had to be in the general context that we were getting ourselves out of our economic crisis. Until the autumn of 1973, when the oil crisis, the world increase in other commodity prices and the home induced increase in inflation through a wage explosion threw the economy finally off-course, increases of a reasonable order in the educational budget remained something for which she must fight.

It was not easy but her attitude reflected her own personal feelings on prudent expenditure and foresight. A typical example of this was a conversation which took place in her private office. One of her senior civil servants was expatiating on the virtues of a new car which he had just bought. 'Good for you,' came Margaret Thatcher's comment, 'but I haven't needed a new one for nearly ten years.'

She had a great belief in the virtues of long-term planning. Decisions had to be made as far as possible on facts not on surmises. Every care had to be taken to find out what the relevant facts were. This meant that she concerned herself particularly with the effect of continuing trends in her field, rather than going for a politically easy answer. It is striking how effective this made her in her arguments with opposition spokesmen on education, like Edward Short and Roy Hattersley, in Parliament.

What she did insist on was candour. She made a practice of going through Parliamentary questions with her junior ministers and her civil servants on any day before questions on education were likely to be reached. At one of these sessions a junior minister asked why a particular answer was being given. 'Because it's the truth,' came the reply. 'But why give more information than has actually been asked for?' he queried. 'Because it's the truth,' the minister answered.

Cabinet ministers have got three principal functions. They have got to run their own particular department. They are responsible for that department, its running and its legislation, to the House. And, by the doctrine of collective responsibility, they are part of the Cabinet team who, under the overall control of the Prime Minister, are responsible for the general strategy of Government.

Predictably, Margaret Thatcher was a painstaking, effective and personally involved departmental chief. She liked to give credit to people who worked with her. When the Department of Education and Science moved during her tenure of office from their premises in Curzon Street to a new block in York Road near Waterloo Station, Lord Belstead, who was then one of her Parliamentary Under-Secretaries, remembers her insisting on having sliding doors put into her own office so that it could be made big enough on occasions by joining it to the next room so that she could personally entertain all the members of her staff who had been involved in the preparatory work for any big Parliamentary debate. She liked to involve herself with the day-to-day work of the department in order to encourage other people. Under Section 68 of the Education Act, 1944, appeals against the decisions of local authorities, particularly in cases on which school a child was allotted to in any particular area, went to the Secretary of State for decision. Margaret Thatcher made a point of deciding these herself and where she made a decision against the appellant would frequently arrange to see the parents personally to explain to them the reasons for this.

Inevitably she was also greatly personally involved with questions of approving schemes that were submitted by the local authorities for the future of secondary education in their areas. She went out of her way to be fair in applying the principles of her own Circular 10/70, consulting with local councils and bearing in mind the interests of the children, rather than doctrinaire principles, in any particular place. When the office was still at Curzon House, a group of her staff who were working late on one particular problem of this kind on which the Minister shortly had to make a decision were surprised when she came in at 10.30 pm at night in full evening dress after an official function to thank them for staying on in order to get the papers ready for the next day and to offer her encouragement.

In her relationships as a Minister with her civil servants she was always professionally very correct and they liked her for it. Unlike some Ministers, in both parties, she would never bawl out one of her staff in public and if she wanted to give anybody a rocket it would always be face to face and in private. With a precise mind herself and used to dealing with business in a clear way, she could get very irritated if things were presented in a muddled or sloppy fashion, but she always tried not to show it publicly.

She was certainly a believer in consultation and in seeing for herself. The DES is a difficult department in that it covers very wide and varied functions. Margaret

Thatcher made a point of getting out of the office and into the regions as much as possible. When regular reviews were held of the improvement programme for school buildings she would frequently cut in and say, 'Oh, but we must have something for that school, I've seen it myself,' producing her own notes; 'they really need that particular facility for the children.' By the end of the three and a half years there was a fair list of schools that she had visited for herself.

Curiously, although she is a scientist by training herself, she was less of a protagonist for abstract science in her public speeches than some of her predecessors who had been arts graduates like Lord Hailsham or Lord Boyle. This was partly because, with her very matter-of-fact approach to politics, she believed in dealing with the practical rather than the abstract. She was interested, however, in comparative matters particularly in the training of scientists, and made a number of official visits abroad in this connection, including ones to India and Romania which broke new ground. While she was at the DES she felt that she must do something to improve her French so as to be able to communicate on matters of this kind. A good many politicians must have felt this, but only a comparatively small number, even of back-benchers, actually got round to taking up the foreign office facilities which are available to help them learn languages. Margaret Thatcher signed on, while Secretary of State, for a crash course, took twice-weekly lessons and then went on learning at home with the aid of a tape recorder. Sometimes this terrific energy could amuse as well as startle those around her. When Sir Alan Bullock, who is a notoriously hard worker, and his committee were appointed to inquire into the teaching of English and reading standards, they were somewhat surprised to be told: 'Lord James's committee managed to report in less than twelve months. Perhaps you could do better than that.'

From the point of view of members of the House of Commons she was readily accessible, which is more than could be said for some of her colleagues in Government, and she listened, which is more than could be said for certain other ones. During the time that one was talking to her, particularly about a constituency matter, one always felt that she was thinking about the matter that was being discussed and did not, as a lot of other senior ministers tend to do, have half her mind on her next appointment.

As a person, she is genuinely interested in other people, makes time to listen to their problems, however mundane, and always looks at them when they are speaking to her. Woe betide, however, a member of Parliament who went to see her on any case without having done his homework, since he was likely to be asked short and extremely penetrating questions.

She can be immensely kind without being sentimental. In the summer of 1972 a ghastly tragedy affected a school party from my constituency when two children from Ipswich who were on an accompanied holiday in Switzerland fell over a cliff on what had been thought to be a comparatively easy walk. One was wearing ankle boots with zip fasteners and synthetic soles, the other casual walking-shoes. Neither of the teachers with them had any previous knowledge of the terrain over which they were going. Anyone who knows the Swiss Alps knows how suddenly precipitous edges can confront one there.

The parents of one of the boys killed came to see me. They showed exemplary courage and fairness but were naturally desperately concerned that everything possible should be done to see that accidents of this type were averted. Accordingly I raised the subject of Safety in Outdoor Pursuits on an adjournment debate which, according to the rather peculiar rules of the House of Commons, came on at the end of the normal day's business.

It was a time of heavy all-night sittings and no-one in the House was getting much sleep. To my total surprise, Margaret Thatcher chose to do the reply to the debate herself at half-past twelve at night, instead of leaving it to a junior minister. She gave a most careful answer to the points which we had raised and said, 'In dealing with hazardous pursuits where the lives of children may be in danger we cannot draw attention too often to the risks that may be involved and to the precautions which must be taken and which can with the right training, help and advice be provided for in advance.'

She had already seen the parents of the boy previously. Now she asked to see them again, however late the hour that the debate finished, and spoke to the mother in a way that I knew she found comforting. This was not a great moment of state, and it is a personal example, but it showed to me most clearly how human Margaret Thatcher can be behind an extremely well-disciplined and business-like exterior.

Another example of her concern for children and their parents was a speech which she made in 1971 in a debate on the subject of career guidance counselling in schools. 'The educational opportunities available—in the schools and in further and higher education—are greater now than they have been at any time in the past. The selection of a career is more complicated than it used to be. New types of jobs with demands for specialist qualifications seem to be coming into being all the time, while the demands for all skills in some trades are diminishing. The need for up-to-date informed guidance is growing all the time. But the schools themselves are going through a process of change which must impose strain on the effectiveness of the services for guidance. The tendency is for secondary schools to become bigger. Unless some conscious effort is made to avoid losing touch with the child as an individual, it is all too easy for the larger units to become impersonal and to fail to meet the individual needs of their pupils.'

Unless some conscious effort is made to avoid losing touch with the child as an individual. These words could almost summarise Margaret Thatcher's concern, as the minister, that the needs of the individual child should come before the system wherever possible. She was determined that the children concerned should have their chance to develop and express themselves and not become submerged in a blueprint of systematic education.

In a major debate on education which took place in answer to a critical opposition motion in February 1973, she summarised her policy as comprising a further advance, giving a better start, better schools, better teaching and a better choice. It was remarkable in fact how much she did achieve. When she summarised government policy on that occasion she did so under five headings, nursery education, school building, teacher training and supply, higher education and overall expenditure. It is worthwhile looking at each category in a little detail.

Nursery education was undoubtedly her greatest achievement in conjunction with the improvements to the primary schools. In his speech on the second reading of the original Education Act of 1944, Lord Butler (then R. A. Butler) had used a very telling expression that 'nursery education would be a form of adult education for the parents as well'. In the 1950s and the early 1960s which was the great age of development in the new universities and the purpose-built secondary schools, nursery schools had become very much the Cinderella of the educational system. Now Margaret Thatcher was to put the clock forward so that the principle of nursery education is firmly established, however little money we have to spend on them in the immediate future. Even Renee Short, the member for Wolverhampton North-East, an unremitting critic of Conservative governments (and frequently of her own) but a champion of the need for nursery education, brought herself to pay tribute to Margaret Thatcher in this regard. What she achieved, in joint consultation with Sir Keith Joseph at the Department of Social Services, was an acceptance of the principle that a combined system of nursery schools and play groups was the best way of involving both parents and children.

As she herself put it in the debate: 'The first major proposal in the White Paper is that within ten years nursery education should become available without charge to children of three and four whose parents wish them to have it. This is an historic step forward which has been widely welcomed. I emphasise that there is no element of compulsion here. We are not proposing to force an earlier school starting age on people who do not want it. We are giving new opportunities to parents if they wish to take advantage of them.' There must be many a harassed mother of a large family who will have considerable cause to bless her as a result, but she was at pains to point out that the purpose of this step forward was to provide for the needs of the child and not just a baby-minding service for the parent. It was a remarkable achievement that in the circumstances of the time, she persuaded her colleagues to agree to earmark building programmes of £30 million in the two years up to 1976 and to plan for an extra 15,000 teachers for this purpose by 1981. Typically, however, she added that Parliament must watch closely to see how the demand developed.

If nursery education had been a Cinderella of the service, provision for primary schools had not exactly been a front-runner under either party over the years. Here again she was determined to give children, particularly children in poorer areas, the best possible start in life. 'The progress already made towards improving the stock of primary schools reflects the Government's determination steadily to get rid of poor and inadequate old buildings,' she stated. Although she was attacked by the Labour front bench on the rather dubious argument of the rate of overall capital expenditure on schools rather than the amount raised to meet particular needs, it was the fact that during the period for 1972–75 primary building programmes were authorised to enable 1,500 old primary schools in England and Wales to be improved or replaced at a cost of £160 million, double the amount approved by the previous government for the last five-year period.

On the question of the supply of teachers Margaret Thatcher was concerned that the main object must be to meet the actual needs which were going to have to be catered for. There was, she believed, a united desire on the part of teachers and parents to secure a reduction in the size of classes. To achieve this for the estimated number of pupils, a projected increase in the overall teaching force of 110,000 teachers was catered for in the period up to 1981, as well as the further 15,000 which would be required for nursery teaching. Provision was made also to increase the number of teachers by a further 20,000 during this period in order to allow for a regular programme of releasing teachers for further training during their careers. With regard to initial training, her policy was to work towards the establishment of a graduate teaching profession. The result was to plan for a teaching force of 510,000 in 1981 as compared to 364,000 in 1971. 'Few professions,' she claimed with some pride, 'have had as great a growth rate as this . . . (but) in the long run I do not believe that the teachers themselves would be grateful if the supply of new recruits to their profession were to grow beyond the point at which local authorities could afford to employ them.'

Higher education proved a controversial aspect of her programme. Once again, she had done her homework thoroughly. 'I must stress,' she said, 'that the government intends to continue to make higher education available for all who are qualified for it and who wish to have it. To translate (this) into numbers up to ten years ahead is difficult because of the uncertainties involved. We know that the raising of the school leaving age (which she had confirmed by Order in Council in 1972, after consultation with the local authorities) or the changing pattern of employment prospects for those completing higher education courses, will make some mark on the trends of numbers but we cannot say with confidence what the effects will be. Even in the short term there are likely to be changes which may or may not indicate a trend. There has already been some slowing-down in the growth of the proportion staying at school to take A-levels and this has not been wholly matched by the growth of this work in the further education sector.

'There are also indications that the demand for higher education from among these qualified may not have been as firmly based as it was in the 1960s. Only recently it was reported that the number of candidates for university courses was lower than that at the same time last year. Applications for places in colleges of education are running at a somewhat lower rate.'

So far, save in a few faculties such as engineering and law, continuing figures have shown that this initial analysis of the situation was correct. Her solution, which was widely welcomed in the educational world, was to provide a coherent merging of the polytechnics, of which she was a formidable champion, and the other colleges to take up half of the further education places estimated to be required by 1981. The amount of recurrent grants was estimated for the universities themselves on an increasing though not a disproportionate number. There was to be a bigger proportion of undergraduates and a smaller proportion of postgraduates. The position of the universities generally was to develop on the basis of a maximum use of limited resources, the facilitation of home-based study and the extension of higher education to areas which were currently compara-tively unprovided for.

In terms of general expenditure it was a programme which was aimed at making the most effective use of the money which was available. Though Labour claimed that her policies, particularly on further education, were restrictive and elitist they have been obliged in fact to adopt many of her costings in the light of the existing economic situation. In the debate in February 1973, Roy Hattersley posed the question whether reductions in overall building expenditure were based on economic or educational reasons and attacked the rate of growth which Margaret Thatcher proposed. Looking back on her period as Secretary for Education, however, there can be no doubt that, compared with what Labour had done themselves between 1964 and 1970, an increase in the educational growth rate for the period between 1973 and 1977, which she obtained (5 per cent in cost terms and at constant prices, compared with a general increase in public expenditure of 2·5 per cent) was a formidable achievement.

Her period at education was notable also for the interest which she showed in a wide variety of subjects which came under the general aegis of her development. During her time as minister, she received the Vernon Report on the needs of the blind and the partially sighted and the Quirk Report on speech therapy. Although she frankly admitted that there was not as much money available to deal with these as she would have liked, she took a keen personal interest in each of the subjects. As well as the James and Bullock Reports, already referred to, she set up an enquiry by Political and Economic Planning (PEP) into the giving of headquarters grants by her ministry to youth organisations and it was a notable feature of her administration that she safeguarded, in terms of continuing cost of living increases, the grants which were made to the central organisations of these bodies. She also established the Business Education Council and the Technical Education Council which have an important part to play in vital fields. In conjunction with the Tizzard Report, she showed a very personal concern with dyslexia and the care of autistic and otherwise handicapped children. She was responsible for the direct grants for artistically specially gifted children to the Yehudi Menuhin School and the Royal Ballet School, currently the only forms of direct grant which are not being phased out.

What she was passionately concerned with was that parents should be given as wide a field of choice as possible for their children and that the intellectually gifted child, whatever his or her background, should be allowed every possible opportunity to make the most of his gifts. For this her opponents, wedded to a programme of rigid egalitarianism, could not forgive her. But she also showed that it was children generally that she cared for and her lengthy period at education, a longer one than most secretaries of state have spent in this department in recent years, although in purely political terms it did not give her the opportunity for a wide variety of cabinet experience, laid the foundations for what succeeding generations can hope to build on.

On educational matters she was obviously extremely vocal in the cabinet. She has been criticised, as has Sir Keith Joseph, another extremely successful departmental minister, for failing to make her voice felt there in other ways. When the Heath government, from the beginning of 1972 onwards, began increasingly to change course from their original position on economic and in particular on monetary policy, it is obvious that neither of these two were particularly happy about the way that things were developing. Ought they therefore to have resigned? It is hard to see what good if anything such a course could have achieved. So long as the Prime Minister remained firmly in the saddle and maintained the general confidence of the Parliamentary Party, as Edward Heath did at this period, there was little that could be done to overrule him while he had the support of a majority of his cabinet. Under the Macmillan government, previous resignations by ministers, on matters over which they disagreed with him (the Marquess of Salisbury over Cyprus and Peter Thorneycroft, Nigel Birch and Enoch Powell, three Treasury ministers, over monetary policy) had had little effect. Under Harold Wilson, the departure of Lord Longford over the delay in deciding to increase the school leaving age had gone largely unnoticed. There was certainly an inner ring to the cabinet under Edward Heath where the centres of power lay. If either Margaret Thatcher or Keith Joseph had quit at this period they would not only have been undermining the position of a Conservative government at a difficult time but they would have been immediately replaced in their departments by other ministers who might have been able to fight for them less than they themselves could.

8

The Leader at Home

How does somebody doing as complex a job as Margaret Thatcher's manage to combine this with her ordinary domestic arrangements? Margaret and Denis Thatcher have been married for nearly twenty-four years, for fifteen of which she has been a Member of Parliament. But she has also had a home to run and two children to bring up.

It helps enormously that Denis Thatcher has himself been a successful business man with a busy career of his own. After being managing director of Atlas Products he became, on successive amalgamations with these firms, a director of Castrol Oil and a director, with special responsibilities in the export field, of Burmah Oil Trading Ltd. Politically he is entirely with his wife. Having stood on his own account at Erith for the Kent County Council in 1951, he has never had any other sort of views. He is what many people would regard as an archetypical Conservative, representing solid traditional values on which he still feels life should be based in the present age.

Denis Thatcher is a decisive personality, with a great deal of character. In his youth he was a first-class rugby player, playing for Old Milhillians as late as 1946, following this with a distinguished career as a rugby referee. He was a member of the London Society of Referees panel for a number of years, served on the Kent panel for seven years and on the panel for top-class games for another three. He still takes a considerable interest in the game, has been treasurer of the London Society and is now a life vice-president. He is an enthusiast about what has been done to speed up rugby, to make it a more open game and to introduce changes in it which have made it more interesting for both the spectators and players. He is also proud of the fact that during the whole of his career, refereeing all types of matches, he was able to extend his authority without having to send players off.

In the summer of 1975 he retired, at sixty, from his full-time appointment with Burmah Oil but he still keeps a number of different interests in various fields. One of these is as chairman of a chemical firm, which is particularly concerned with treating the turf for sports stadia—having been involved with the playing areas for clubs like Derby County at the Baseball Ground and Leicester City at Filbert Street he admits to being nearly as interested in watching association football on television now as he is with his own game. He is also an enthusiastic sailor, crewing with the Island Cruising Club, and a keen golfer.

Denis Thatcher is the sort of person to whom it would never even remotely enter his mind to be jealous of his wife's career. He is a great believer in people being able to do their own thing and, like his wife, believes that they should do anything to which they turn their hands to the utmost of their ability. To him loyalty is an all-important virtue whether it is on a personal basis or directed towards whatever firm or cause one works for.

For a number of years the Thatchers have coped with running two houses, one in London for work reasons and one in Kent so that the children could have the opportunity of being brought up in the country. When they were first married their Kent home was at Farnborough, where between them they created a garden of which they were very proud. Later they moved to a house called The Mount at Lamberhurst which had a large but very over-run garden. Together, to save labour, they re-planned this so as to reduce a lot of the orchard and have more lawn and they worked to give it a character of its own. More recently, they have moved into a flat, part of a house also at Lamberhurst, which is easier to run, and their gardening activities, to which both are devoted, are restricted to the patch behind their London home at Flood Street, Chelsea. They did manage to trans- plant some of their favourite shrubs there, however, including a rhododendron of which both are extremely proud. Margaret Thatcher insisted on taking with them all their watering-cans from the bigger garden but Denis Thatcher quietly ignores her advice on using these and copes cheerfully with a hose instead.

One casualty of the move was Margaret Thatcher's piano, for which there was insufficient room in either the Lamberhurst flat or at Chelsea. Although they miss this they are both still keen musicians and like to go to the opera and to concerts, though they find that it is one of the disadvantages of her job as Leader of the Opposition that it leaves them less time to go to Covent Garden or Glynde- bourne. They are also enthusiastic theatre-goers, which is a taste they share with their children. When they were first married they used to go to the cinema quite a lot but today they find this more difficult, though the whole family tends to go on the spur of the moment to their local London cinema round the corner in the King's Road.

Their television-watching tends to be selective. Margaret Thatcher generally wants to watch the news and current affairs programmes and the children have got used to her rushing into the house asking 'When's the news?', to which the whole family replies 'At nine o'clock, mum!' She can sometimes be inveigled into watching the Sunday night film but often has to break into this to get back to her official papers! At Lamberhurst they have got a black and white set, which can only get one channel, much to the annoyance of Mark and Carol, their children, who prefer watching on colour in London.

Although sport is more a part of Denis Thatcher's life than it is of Margaret Thatcher's, the whole family shares a keen interest in ski-ing. For a number of years they used to ski at the same village in Switzerland, Lenzerheider in the Glisons, where the children knew all the local people and always had the same guides and instructor each winter. They also learnt to ride well and Margaret Thatcher herself is an intermittent but not particularly proficient tennis player.

Travel they enjoy enormously. In connection with his job, Denis Thatcher had to do a great deal of travelling in America, in Africa and the Far East. Each of them took a strong view, however, about wives accompanying their husbands on business expenses unless there was a valid reason for this, and Margaret Thatcher was not generally able to go with him even if her Parliamentary duties would have allowed time for her to do so. Consequently, when Denis Thatcher goes with his wife on her official visits abroad he makes a point of not being under any obligation regarding his own expenses on the trips.

Neither of them is particularly good at languages, though Margaret Thatcher managed to learn sufficiently fluent French from her Foreign Office course when she was at the Department of Education and Science to be able to more than hold her own on her first official visit to President Giscard d'Estaing. She also created quite an impression on her first visit to the European Parliament by being able to follow without always having to resort to simultaneous translation.

Whenever possible on her trips inside the United Kingdom, Denis Thatcher likes to go with her and this is popular with the constituencies. He finds that he has an additional function on these occasions since although she is invariably punctual about getting to an appointment (not one of her immediate predecessor's best-known virtues!) she tends to get interested and involved in what she is doing and to over-run the time which has been allotted at any particular place. It is one of his jobs to jog her elbow quietly and make sure that she gets off to the next place where she is expected.

She puts a great deal into her speeches and tends to get rather worked up before one. Speaking at public meetings is something she regards as very important since it brings her into direct contact with people. She has mixed views about the

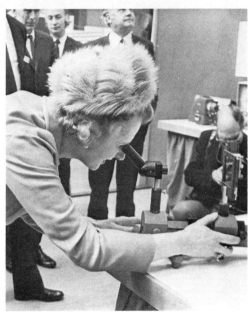

bove Margaret Thatcher, Minister of
ducation, listens as schoolchildren use
e revolutionary Talking Page teaching
stem in 1971

Above Margaret Thatcher at the Physics Exhibition at Alexandra Palace, London, in March
1972

Margaret Thatcher in 1969 shortly after succeeding Sir Edward Boyle as Shadow Minister Education

Above Mrs Thatcher with her husband Denis and their children Mark and Carol at their home in Lamberhurst, Kent in 1970

Left With Princess Margaret at a Buckingham Palace Garden Party for exchange teachers in 1972

Below Mrs Thatcher in her new office which she designed herself, when the Education Department moved to Elizabeth House near Waterloo Station

Right The Minister of Education, Mrs Margaret Thatcher, with *(left)* Norman St John Stevas, welcome Lord Sandford, the new Parliamentary Under-Secretary of Education, on his arrival to take up his new post

Above Margaret Thatcher with William Whitelaw during the leadership election contest, 1975

Left Mrs Thatcher jubilant after hearing the result of the first ballot for the leadership

The new Tory leader at her first Press Conference

Left Margaret Thatcher outsic her Chelsea home after her vi tory in the Conservative Par leadership election

Left Mr and Mrs Denis Tha cher, 1975

effect of television on politics in this country since although she feels that it is obviously a very important medium she also feels that it can have the effect of dehumanising politics and making people distrust politicians who use television with too easy a facility. It is vitally important in her view that the real issues should come over and they do not always do so on the screen, which sometimes trivialises essential matters.

Although her speaking trips in various parts of Britain do not generally last more than a few days at a time, they do entail going to a large number of different functions and being constantly exposed to photographers, reporters and television cameras. To cope with this Margaret Thatcher has to take with her a more extensive wardrobe than a male politician and she has had a specially constructed suitcase made to help with this to facilitate quick changes. She still looks after her own clothes and deals with things like sewing on buttons for herself. Naturally, what she wears attracts a good deal of feminine interest but one thing that she is rigidly against is any form of commercial sponsorship with her clothes. She buys all of these at normal retail prices. The only concession she will accept is her hairdresser opening his salon for her early, sometimes before she goes off for a heavy schedule of functions. Having very fine hair, which blows about easily, she needs to have it done regularly.

She is a feminist but not in a militant sense. She merely regards it as perfectly natural that women should be able to do the same jobs that men can do in an increasing number of fields and she takes a good deal of pride in what they are able to achieve. Politically, she expects no sort of quarter or special treatment because she is a woman, but she does become angry if men try to talk down to their female colleagues in any circumstances or to treat them in any other way than they would each other. She becomes particularly irritated at the comparatively small number of women who have still come to the top in careers like politics and the law considering the wealth of talent that is available. She is also irritated if a woman feels that she cannot do what she wishes in terms of a career because she gets too tied down by household chores. To this end she has taken great pains with organising her own life to allow herself scope to have an effective career.

The Thatchers do not now have any living-in help in London but when the children were younger they were lucky in being able to have a nanny, who helped to look after them and later helped to run the household in the larger house at Lamberhurst. Today they have a number of people about the Flood Street house who help Margaret Thatcher to cope, including a personal secretary who comes in most mornings and a number of ladies who come in 'to oblige', but they have no permanent housekeeper.

Up till fairly recently Margaret Thatcher did most of her own shopping. She

F

still buys all her own clothes but gets a certain amount of assistance from various people with the household shopping in London and Denis Thatcher tends to do most of the shopping for Kent (one reason, he guesses, why she kept the now celebrated stock of tinned foods!). She is a good shopper and knows what she wants and minds about quality and consumer choice. She is particularly good at buying presents, which she specially enjoys, and likes surprising her family, though she minds very much about buying the right present for each one and for her staff. Luckily she knows what she wants to buy, generally in advance, and she has been known to get the whole of her Christmas shopping done in less than three hours.

She is personally an extremely good cook, although she does not get much time for it now. It is a real hobby with her and she loves doing it. At Flood Street she has a modern, labour-saving kitchen where she has always enjoyed both experimenting with dishes and cooking classic, traditional ones. At Downing Street she will probably be the first Prime Minister to be able to cast a really experienced eye over the official entertaining. She is a methodical cook and likes to take trouble about what she is preparing but she hates to be hurried when she is getting a meal ready and she does like people to be on time to eat it.

Both the Thatchers like entertaining and find it annoying that they can do less of it than they used to be able to do. Margaret Thatcher is a considerate hostess who likes to see that her guests are taken care of. Whenever possible they like to see their own friends and not just political colleagues. Being tied to the House of Commons or official engagements is a restriction from this point of view and she has reluctantly come to use outside caterers or ready-prepared food on occasions when she does have a supper party which she personally finds irritating.

Like every politician she is subject to the normal vagaries of Parliamentary life but she minds about being on time and she has a rooted objection to breaking engagements. After she became the Leader of the Opposition, the producer of the BBC *Any Questions* programme was surprised to find that she was the first Party Leader of either of the major parties to appear on it. She had simply accepted the invitation before her appointment and was unwilling to break it whatever the circumstances.

Finding opportunities to get right away from the political scene is more difficult for her now than it used to be. This is one reason why the whole family likes to go to Kent, where Margaret Thatcher can be relatively free of the telephone, and they can all wear old clothes and relax on their own.

When they moved from The Mount at Lamberhurst they got rid of a number of their larger pieces of furniture but Flood Street has always been furnished with antiques that they have bought up and down the country and they have moved larger items to London for which there is no room at the flat in Kent. Margaret Thatcher herself is particularly interested in porcelain and pottery and she has recently formed an interest in Chinese pictures which she has started to collect. Fortunately, both she and Denis Thatcher have the same sort of tastes in decorating a house. They work well together on painting and wall-papering and both of them are good with their hands, though Denis Thatcher prefers to consider himself as the plasterer's mate. Margaret Thatcher herself likes doing things about the house like mending shelves or changing fuses.

She is personally very interested in pictures and was amused at the recent controversy over Ruskin Spear's highly unattractive picture of her at the Royal Academy. Although the artist himself seemed to think that she had no right to say so, what did irritate her was that he had done the portrait, without any sittings, from press photographs and without his having contact of any kind with his subject. The kind of painter she does admire very much is the careful craftsman like Annigoni. She is also very pleased with a portrait bust which has been done of her by a woman sculptor who lives in her constituency.

Books play a large part in both their lives. Although official papers take up a good deal of her time as far as her reading matter is concerned and Denis Thatcher has always had to read a good deal of technical material to keep up with developments in the petrochemical industry, they both like reading history and political biographies. They enjoy discussing together books which they happen to be reading. Margaret Thatcher also likes going back to her old favourites and generally keeps an anthology of poetry in their bedroom. When they go on holiday they like to read fiction and take thrillers like Simenon with them as well.

Their chief interest has always been the children. Although it is always difficult for any politician, or any successful industrialist for that matter, to find as much time as they would like to have to spend with their family they have always made a point of this. Both the children were given a down-to-earth upbringing and were never allowed to get away with things unnecessarily. Both their parents in fact have healthy, old-fashioned firm views about bringing up children and seeing that they have good manners, and feel that this is the best way to make them into civilised individuals. They are enormously proud of how both the twins, now aged twenty-two, have developed. Mark, who went to school at Harrow, was the public schools racquets champion while he was there and is now studying to qualify as an accountant. Carol, or Carol Jane as the family tend to call her, went to Queenswood School in Hertfordshire and from there to St Paul's. She has inherited both her mother's looks and her legal brain and is now doing her articles with a firm of solicitors at Chichester. Both the children have minds of their own and have inherited their parents' practical dispositions.

They are a well-balanced family and an extremely close one. Politics is always a difficult life for a family because of the amount of time which it takes up, but the Thatchers seem to be able to cope with these problems better than most. They do sometimes look back a little ruefully to the years that she was at the bar, however, because of the amount of extra time that it allowed them to spend together in the evenings.

Inevitably she now has to work an immensely long day. They are generally up by 7 o'clock and Margaret Thatcher still cooks breakfast herself for whichever of the family are at home. She has usually left for the House of Commons by about half-past ten and often has to stay there until a late hour in the evening. Since she has been Leader of the Opposition she has been provided with an official car but before that used to drive herself to work. She is a good driver but when she and Denis Thatcher are going out together it is usually he, by common consent, who drives. Like many other politicians she has the facility of being able to work on train journeys.

In addition to her duties as Leader there is still, of course, a great deal of time to be spent in the constituency. When she was a junior minister in the Macmillan government, and had a majority of more than 15,000 at Finchley at the time before the size of the constituency was cut down, Harold Macmillan used to greet her on the front bench by saying, 'Hullo, are you still as busy as ever with nursing that highly marginal seat of yours?' Denis Thatcher likes going with her to constituency engagements and always accompanies her to the count at election times. As a trained cost and works man he takes his slide-rule with him and can usually work out what her majority is going to be long before she or her agent have any idea how she has fared.

Once she has dealt with them she hates the clutter which papers involve. She does not keep a personal diary, keeps no copies of her personal letters although she writes a lot and tears up the drafts of her speeches as soon as these have been typed. From this point of view she is the biographer's nightmare and unlike most politicians there is no sort of Margaret Thatcher archive available. She is one potential Prime Minister who is highly unlikely to write her memoirs!

Like most politicians there must be moments when she feels that she would like to be doing something less totally time-consuming but she has always regarded it as her duty to get on with what she has set her hand to. Although she never expected to become the Leader when she went into politics, she has not allowed herself to become alarmed or deterred by the prospect of becoming the first woman Prime Minister. One thing that she does agree with Harold Wilson over is his decision to treat 10 Downing Street as the Prime Minister's official office and headquarters and the benefits of keeping a family home at the same time, rather than 'living on top of the shop'!

She will be the most approachable Prime Minister that there has been for many years. Denis Thatcher sometimes worries about the amount of time that she is willing to give to the job and the number of engagements she has always been ready to take on but he knows that she feels this is right and there is nothing he can do to dissuade her from this.

Margaret Thatcher is essentially a happy person and likes what she is doing and this is something which communicates itself to people around her. This is an important aspect of her character since, although the problems facing her as a future Prime Minister are going to be immense, she is able to take a balanced view of these. What will certainly not happen is that she will let them deter or depress her. She would have been good at and probably gone to the top in whatever profession she followed. She would certainly have made an excellent judge and might even have become the first female member of the Bench in that hitherto exclusively male enclave, the Chancery Division. But it is what she is doing and not what she has become that is the real interest to her. It is her quality of being able to throw herself into what she is doing at the time that makes so many people feel fond of her.

Fergus Montgomery, her PPS, and his wife often have her to stay when she is on speaking tours in the north-west near his constituency of Altrincham and Sale in Cheshire. The first time she went there after she became Leader the press wanted to know what special arrangements would be made for her visit. Were they, one journalist asked, going to have the spare room re-decorated blue in her honour? Would they, another one wanted to know, be laying on special menus for her visit? How were they going to entertain her? 'I expect,' Joyce Montgomery told these slightly disappointed correspondents, 'that she will come and have scrambled eggs with us in the kitchen after the meeting because that is what she usually does when she comes here.'

She cannot bear fuss and bother about this kind of thing and it is one thing that does irritate her particularly if the people making the arrangements for her try to make her programme too formal. It is extraordinary how many people from all periods of her life remember her quite clearly years afterwards. Edward Gardner, now the Member of Parliament for the South Fylde of Lancashire, was her immediate successor as candidate at Erith and Crayford, when the Dartford constituency was divided into two. Some time after he was selected there he met Denis Thatcher, who asked him how he was getting on. 'There's only one thing I do find difficult,' Ted Gardner replied; 'they will all keep on talking about Margaret Roberts there.'

Being a politician, particularly a top politician, can be an extremely lonely life. Some people in the circumstances become interested, others tend to play to the gallery or become self-important. Margaret Thatcher's approach to being Prime Minister will, I think, be very like the way in which she runs her domestic arrangements, in a sensible, friendly and matter-of-fact approach. However good you are in politics it is never worth it if you end up by complicating your own life so that you stop enjoying things. To be a successful woman politician and run a family takes thought and takes care. Anyone who can cope with life as well as she does has had a pretty good apprenticeship for the top political job of all.

9

Conversation at Wilton Street

A few days after Margaret Thatcher's election as leader of the Tory Party a lady was having her hair done at a ladies hairdressers in Ipswich. A teenager came in and sat down in the next chair. 'What style does madam want?' inquired the assistant. 'I want a Margaret Thatcher,' the girl firmly replied.

Within a short time of coming onto the centre of the stage she had already undoubtedly caught the imagination of the public. People as a whole are interested in her. They are interested in who she is and what she stands for to a greater degree than with any political figure for years.

Her public appearances have a real charisma about them. In Scotland, in the North of England, in the Midlands, in Wales, the very areas where her Labour critics suggested that she would go down least well, she has been received with tremendous enthusiasm. In Scotland, particularly, where politicians from south of the border have not exactly been at a premium in recent years, people have poured out to see her and she has been greeted with real and spontaneous warmth. In Dundee, for instance, a city currently divided largely between the Labour and the Scottish Nationalist parties, the crowd that gathered on her visit carried home-made banners outside the Caird Hall with messages like: 'We are for Margaret Thatcher, Harold Wilson cannot match her' and 'We love you, Maggie'. Her reception has been the same all over the place, at Cardiff, at Glasgow, at Edinburgh, at Aberystwyth, at Derby, at Bolton, at Montrose.

The press, inevitably, has dismissed this as a honeymoon period. Some Conservatives, particularly the immediate supporters of Edward Heath, have been equally sceptical. Labour organisers have been frankly worried by this reaction and have tried to write it off as a flash in the pan. But the fact remains that people do want to see the Tory leader, that she is generating affection on a quite unprecedented level.

Political commentators have tried to analyse this and to explain its significance in short-term psephological terms. They have argued that she is a woman, which helps, that she is an extremely good-looking one, which certainly helps, and that she is at the moment exercising a film-star attraction but that in the long run she will be treated as just any other political leader.

There is more to these welcomes, however, than simply curiosity about a new public figure on the scene. There is a spontaneity, a friendliness and, above all, a directness about Margaret Thatcher which appeals fundamentally to people. Britain has been through a bad time in the last few years. The press, the electors themselves, even the politicians have got used to repeating that politics as such have fallen low in the public estimation. The voters have grown tired, it has been said with some truth, of politicians knocking each other on their television screens. They are disillusioned with political figures who have tried to evade the issues, with policies that have been inadequately explained to them, with sectionalism and factionalism in the country's affairs. Democracy, it is being increasingly suggested, is no longer a tenable system in this country as such.

There is already a feeling that Margaret Thatcher has the capacity to break through this feeling of disillusion. People can sense her honesty and her genuine and immediate concern with what politics means for ordinary people's lives. There is a real if largely unspoken hope that she can prove the catalyst to bring a return to a saner state of things.

It is interesting in this regard to compare the speech which she made on becoming the leader of the Conservative party with the one made by her father thirty years before on accepting the mayoralty at Grantham. It is particularly significant to realise that this similarity is entirely unconscious. Unlike her sister Muriel, who tends to keep family records, Margaret Thatcher does not keep press cuttings about her family or herself. She does not watch herself, even in a replay, on television, on the basis that once a broadcast has gone out there is nothing more that she can do about it. The similarity between her father's ideas and her own is therefore based entirely on a similarity between their personalities. Alfred Roberts's concern was to seek to represent the needs of the community as a whole. The same is true of Margaret Thatcher.

That does not mean that she can possibly seek to please everybody. Perhaps politicians as a whole have sought too hard to please. The role of the demagogue and the role of the dictator are equally dangerous in contemporary society. What is important is the down-to-earth quality which she represents. If politics is to mean anything at all, it must stand for a free and constant choice in a democracy.

She is an enormously hard worker and by hard work has been able to achieve a good deal. But she has never felt this kind of achievement to be an end in itself.

This is where her Methodist upbringing has been of great significance, the feeling that one has been brought into the world not just to do the best by oneself but to try to serve other people as well.

Unlike many other politicians she is remarkably unconcerned with her own image or with the impression that she makes. Other political figures who have been of significance in the last decade, Harold Wilson, Edward Heath, Enoch Powell and Anthony Wedgwood Benn, for instance, have been consistently concerned with the projection of their own personalities. Margaret Thatcher is supremely unconcerned with this. She has, for example, given herself one of the shortest entries printed in the current edition of *Who's Who*. I very much doubt if she bothers to read even a small proportion of the biographical material that is written about her in the press or elsewhere. It is doing things that matters.

She has taught herself to be very self-disciplined and enormously resistant. She is not at all introverted. Her agent, Ray Langston, describes her tremendous buoyancy, how quickly she can rise to an occasion whatever the difficulties. She can come down to deal with a constituency problem the following morning even after she had been up all night on a late sitting of the House of Commons, and give it her entire attention. Rarely for a politician, she does not let herself get blown off course by any personal set-back. If she had lost the leadership election in 1975, as she fully thought she might, right up to the last moment, I believe that she would have come back and played whatever role the party had needed of her.

She was accused at the time of the leadership contest of being influenced by personal ambition. As one leading Labour politician put it, it was a question of the dog seeing the rabbit and taking its chance. This is, I think, an entire misunderstanding of her nature. A personally ambitious politician in that sense would hardly have stayed in the same job, however important, from 1970 to 1974 without becoming restive, and would certainly not have accepted the place as number two to Robert Carr in opposition. A personally ambitious politician would have been inclined to weigh up the consequences much more carefully and calculate the chances before letting her name go forward against Edward Heath.

It is the results of the job which interest her much more than the power or the position which it involves. What she is really interested in is what can be achieved in office and not the right to hold office itself.

As Leader of the Opposition she has remained totally approachable to other members when they want to see her. It is a characteristic which she has always had. When she was shadow minister for the Environment in 1974, Peter Morrison, the member for Chester, came up to her in the division lobby at the House of Commons and asked if he might come and see her about a rating question which was affecting his constituency. 'There's no time like the present,' she replied, and immediately sat down with him to discuss the problem.

She likes to go to the tea room in the House so as to be available to colleagues with as little fuss as possible. During a working meal she has a rather endearing habit of listening to what the person sitting next to her is saying with complete concentration and then suddenly remembering that she is hungry and eating up her food in a hurry before it gets taken away.

She likes to go on taking an interest in people she has met or places that she has been to. Sir Bill Elliot, the member for Newcastle (North), has in his constituency a well-known school for handicapped children, the Northern Counties School for the Deaf. Like other ministers for Education she went up to speak there on Speech Day. Before going there she asked him all about the school and he gave her a good many details. When the day came she had obviously made a tremendous effort both to look more beautifully turned out than her usual self and to prepare a special speech. After it was over, although she had another engagement at Middlesbrough, she asked the Chairman of the Governors if she might meet as many of the parents and children as possible and stayed as long as she could, although she was continually urged to hurry up by the people responsible for her programme.

Some time later, when she was already Leader of the party, Bill Elliot reminded her of this occasion and told her that he had a party coming down from the school to visit the House the following week. 'When are they coming?' she immediately asked. 'Would you like me to see them?' 'Of course,' he said. 'Then would you ask Fergus Montgomery (her PPS) to fix it up?' At 12.00 pm they were due at the St Stephen's entrance and at 12.00 precisely Margaret Thatcher appeared there. A small girl came up and explained to her with some difficulty because of her disability that she could remember her coming to the school. Margaret Thatcher was genuinely delighted.

Her attitude towards political life is very well balanced. Some ministers make a fetish of office and tend to become unapproachable. Others tend to spend a lot of time in the Smoking Room of the House of Commons building up a power base for themselves. Margaret Thatcher has always been conscious that she has a life of her own outside politics and has generally managed with some success to keep her own life with her family and friends, her interests in music and the theatre, separate so that she does not become too wholly engulfed in a political atmosphere.

However busy she is, she certainly does not allow politics to interfere too much with her own life. A friend of the Thatchers gave a good example of this. A neighbour of theirs in Chelsea was suddenly taken ill. She had young children at home, and animals, and her husband had already gone off to his work. Everybody was wringing their hands and wondering what to do next when suddenly Margaret Thatcher, who had been told about the difficulties, arrived. She arranged to take the children to their grandparents and to put the dogs in kennels temporarily, put a casserole in the oven for the husband when he came home, left instructions for him how to deal with this and went off to the House of Commmons for her day's engagements. Anybody else, perhaps, could have done this if they had the organising ability but she is essentially the sort of person who can deal with a crisis quietly, efficiently and without a fuss.

She has got, fortunately for her, a great deal of personal stamina, which certainly belies her rather fragile appearance. Since the days in Dartford when she got used to working almost round the clock, she has maintained the ability to get by on only a few hours' sleep. During the long sessions of voting on the Industrial Relations Bill and the European Communities Bill it has always been surprising how fresh she managed to look in the division lobbies even in the small hours of the morning. After one all-night sitting she said good-night to her PPS Fergus Montgomery, when she left the House at about 6.00 am. 'Well,' she said, 'see you at the meeting at the department at 10.00 am,' and went off home, apparently unconcerned.

One of the reasons that she can work such long hours without ill effect is that she knows how to relax. Although she is meticulous about taking home official papers to work on and will work late on these or on preparing a speech, she can switch her mind off when she has finished and enjoy herself in her other interests.

The fact that she has been fundamentally involved with serious problems means that many people have tended to think of Margaret Thatcher as a wholly serious person. A woman party leader does not have the same opportunities to unwind in public, particularly in front of the television camera, as a male one does, for example in the kind of speeches that she makes at public dinners or when she appears at sporting occasions. She has to be more careful than her male counterparts, for instance, about the kind of remarks that she makes on occasions like this. From her background Margaret Thatcher is inclined to be naturally conscious of the need to maintain certain standards and it would not be welcome with many people if she did not.

She can, however, be very entertaining company. Lord Reigate (formerly Sir John Vaughan-Morgan and a Conservative minister) gives a good example of this. In 1970 when she became Secretary for Education he went up to congratulate her and gave her a warm kiss. 'Do you know,' he said, 'you're the first Secretary of State for Education and Science that I've ever kissed.' (All her immediate predecessors in the job had been male.) 'I hope,' she replied, 'I'm the first one you've ever wanted to.' She can be amusingly frank on occasions. The author's younger son, who was then nine, can still remember being teased by her one day when brought to lunch at the canteen in the House of Commons and introduced to her. She told him that he had got the dirtiest face she had ever seen in the Palace of Westminster. Generally when grown-ups talk to children in this sort of way they can be either annoying or patronising. She did it so nicely and with such a real sense of fun that he adored her.

She is good with people because she genuinely likes them. However busy she may be she will always make time to talk to people properly. She is one of the top politicians who is genuinely always sensitive to other people's feelings and hates to hurt them. This does not mean that she cannot be quite sharp on occasions but always discreetly and always directly to the individual concerned. She can be extremely thoughtful about people with whom she is concerned. Mrs Bicker, who worked for her family in Grantham for years, still talks with excitement about the day when Margaret Thatcher came back to open some extensions to the Kesteven Girls School, but as a distinguished old girl and as the education minister. Later the same afternoon there was a knock on her door and a small girl appeared carrying an enormous bunch of red roses. 'Mrs Thatcher thought you might like to have these,' she said. It was the bouquet that she had been presented with at the ceremony that morning.

She likes to identify with people in any particular situation. In 1972 she went to open a new primary school in Ipswich, one of the hundreds of engagements of this sort that she must have undertaken up and down the country. At the lunch afterwards she made a speech and suddenly spotted the Ipswich MP's twelve-year-old daughter in the room. 'I'm so glad that the member's daughter is here on this occasion,' she said in her speech. 'It reminds me of the times that I used to go to things like this with my father. It's good to get involved at that age.'

Having a happy family life of her own is very important to her. She has always felt, rightly, that she and her husband and their children were entitled to a family life of their own, whatever the outside pressures. She was irritated by the press accounts of her getting up at 6.30 am to cook the family breakfast even after she became leader because it seemed to her to be such a normal thing to do.

She has never personally courted publicity, except in terms of ideas which she believed in, and for this reason, until 1974, she was one of the publicly least well-known of the Tory leaders. Curiously, despite her formidable reputation in Parliament, this led some sectors of the press to discount her chances in the leadership contest.

It must also have been a disadvantage at this stage that she was a woman. It has always taken the political parties as such some time to adapt to the changes in national life that go on around them, and this applies to all the major parties.

Doubts were expressed at first whether a woman could in fact be an effective leader. Now that it has happened and she has become established as the Conservative leader, nothing could seem more natural.

Interestingly, with her election to the leadership, her public appearance has to some extent subtly changed. Her clothes have always tended to be formalised and rather stylised, and she is perhaps more stylish than many people's idea of a politician. Not only has she visibly become more relaxed in public in general, as she has felt the warmth of her reception, but she has taken to wearing still very becoming but rather more simple outfits.

Her predilection for wearing hats was at one time a cartoonist's dream. Apart from the fact that she likes hats herself and takes pleasure in choosing them, there is also a good reason for her wearing them so often since they tend to keep her hair tidy in going from one engagement to another.

Her television appearances have become increasingly effective. Although it is the content rather than the manner of these with which she is basically concerned, she is good on television and it is a medium which is suited to her for a number of reasons. As far as political broadcasts on television are concerned, these best suit simple straightforward argument and presentation of the facts and this has always been her style. She has always favoured a quietly reasoned rather than a didactic or abrasive manner of argument and she dislikes personal invective. All this creates the genuine impression that she is speaking directly to people in their own homes and not addressing them like a mass meeting.

It is noticeable that many Socialists, though they strongly disagree with her ideas and the force with which she holds them, find it difficult to dislike her personally. This particularly applies to Socialist Members of Parliament. She can be sharp and even cutting in debate but because she does not descend to personalities or animosity this is not resented.

Her voice is a very clear one and she always speaks with great precision. Basically you need to see her as well as hear her to feel the full warmth of her personality and this makes her better on television than she is on sound radio.

In the House of Commons she has obviously got to overcome certain difficulties. She can be a powerful speaker in debate and is extremely good at using pauses to underline her points in putting forward her case. Where at present this is not so easy is when the going in the House gets particularly rowdy. A woman cannot shout down barracking from the other side in quite the same way as a man can, without losing some of her poise. She has to rely therefore on force of personality rather than physical weight when it comes to overcoming a determined crescendo of noise from the other benches.

It is a situation which she is finding increasingly easy to handle as she grows more accustomed to being a Front Bench leader. There is no doubt that she has got the necessary *gravitas* to enable her to dominate the House. There is also another factor. The recent introduction of broadcasts of Parliamentary proceedings, particularly question time, has not exactly impressed the public with regard to the sheer weight of noise and interruption to which members have grown used. This may before long have an important effect on changing the style of the House in this regard, since most MPs are very conscious of public reaction.

Any leader depends to a very considerable degree on the loyalty of his or her own supporters. Here Margaret Thatcher is in a position both of considerable strength and of some immediate embarrassment. As leader of her party she is very much the spontaneous creation of her own backbenchers and she carries with her the overwhelming support of the majority of the Parliamentary party. As a matter of historical precedent, she is in fact the first leader of the Conservative Party who has emerged not through consultation with the inner establishment and then a process of election but by a strong feeling on the part of individual back-bench members that she was the person that they wanted to lead them, even though she had originally come on the scene considered as something of an outsider in the race. But general feeling in the party is that she is a good choice.

Unfortunately, there are some members of the Parliamentary party, though they are quite a small group, who have not been prepared to accept the realities of her election, however democratic its form and however much it represented the wish of the majority of members. Particularly unhappily her relations with Edward Heath himself have become a highly publicised and sensitive area.

The position has been highlighted by the controversy which has arisen about her visit to him at his house at Wilton Street, London, shortly after she succeeded to the Leadership. On the night of the election she was asked whether she intended to offer a place in her shadow cabinet to the former Leader and she indicated that she very much hoped that he would serve in it.

The world's press was now waiting to see what would happen and a fair sprinkling of it was waiting outside Edward Heath's house when she arrived there. On any basis the visit must have been an extremely difficult one. Heath, who has always tended to be a lonely figure, had centred his life completely on politics and was deeply hurt by what he felt to be his rejection. Margaret Thatcher was embarrassed for him, though she was well aware that politics is a hard world. She had obviously expected that the meeting might be difficult. When it took place it turned out to be almost monosyllabic as far as he was concerned.

She had clearly gone to Wilton Street for a purpose. It was in her interest and in the interests of the party as a whole that he should be persuaded to agree to continue to serve on the Front Bench. On the comparatively recent precedent of

Sir Alec Douglas-Home, who agreed to stay on in Edward Heath's own Shadow Cabinet after the latter took over from him, he would obviously be entitled, if he was willing to continue to serve, to suggest that he should fill a senior post of his own choice.

In the emotionally charged atmosphere of this meeting Edward Heath may have felt too hurt to be able to take in just what was being put to him. At her host's volition the conversation turned out to be extremely short. Whatever she tried to put to him was met by a stony and negative reply. The former Leader and the new Leader of the Conservative Party had gone into the first-floor sitting-room at Heath's home and sat down there. Margaret Thatcher began by explaining that she wanted Edward Heath to continue to serve with her.

'*Shan't*,' came the discouraging answer.

Undeterred, she started to ask him to indicate what part he was now willing to take.

'*Won't*,' he cut in.

'*What can I say?*' she said to him.

'*There is nothing to say*,' he replied.

They sat for a time in oppressive silence. Taken aback by how things had developed she silently got up and left the room.

After less than five minutes she found herself downstairs again in the hall. She had to face going out to meet the press with what they would inevitably read into so brief a visit and so rapid a departure. To save everybody's face she stayed in Heath's house for another quarter-of-an-hour talking to Sir Timothy Kitson, Heath's PPS. Then she left, and smiled a 'no comment' at the cameras and newsmen.

Edward Heath has now said several months later that no approach was in fact made to him at this meeting and no job was offered. When it was announced at the time in nearly every newspaper that Margaret Thatcher *had* asked him to join her and that he had refused, no attempt was then made by him or anybody else on his behalf to suggest that this was anything other than accurate. When the suggestion was ultimately made in the late summer to this effect Airey Neave, as head of her private office, went on record on her behalf immediately to state that an offer *had* been made. Everything in the surrounding circumstances supports him as being correct.

During the latter part of Heath's years in office and during 1974 relations between the two of them had certainly not appeared to be particularly easy. When Margaret Thatcher became the Leader of the Party and succeeded him as Leader of the Opposition, Edward Heath not only obviously resented it but particularly resented being replaced by her. Unfortunately, in consequence, the general tenor of his attitude towards her since her election seems to have been at variance with the dignified role which he played when the question of the Leadership first came under consideration. It was also a very different scene from what happened in the case of his own succession to Sir Alec Douglas-Home in what were potentially equally difficult circumstances. If Edward Heath had been prepared to serve again, either immediately or at a later date, on the Front Bench, he would have confirmed for himself a position of considerable authority in the Party. As it is, what has happened, both in February and since, has lost him a good deal of respect and admiration even among his former close colleagues.

The continuance of what has been termed a Heath group in the Parliamentary party, 'the Norman Shaw cabal', so-called because of the recently converted Parliamentary building where the former Leader and several of his immediate supporters have their offices, was obviously an irritant during the first months of her Leadership. The attitude of Edward Heath himself has, sadly, only probably served to diminish his own reputation with his colleagues who have grown increasingly irritated with his personal rejection of Margaret Thatcher's leadership, such as the occasion in the House itself when she complimented him on the part which he had played in the successful EEC Referendum Campaign and he studiedly turned his head away and ignored the compliment—and her. The fact that he has chosen locations like Madrid and Zurich to make speeches criticising his former colleagues has not exactly endeared him to them either. There are a number of leading politicians who supported Edward Heath in the Leadership election and who are now undoubtedly behind Margaret Thatcher as a result.

Three things are quite clear. She is now firmly in the saddle, with the support of the Party in Parliament and the constituencies. Her policies are beginning to make a real impact on the country, as the result of the West Woolwich by-election showed. Any attempt by the ex-Leader to challenge her leadership in the autumn, though it would be perfectly valid under the terms of the new procedure, could only now result in his own humiliation, which many of the people who have previously regarded him with admiration would deeply regret.

During her first few months, criticism was levelled at her with regard to the 'low profile' that she was being said to adopt in Opposition. In a much-publicised phrase, Harold Wilson sneeringly spoke of 'the reluctant debutante coming at last to the despatch box'. Events, however, have proved her perfectly right. It would have been wrong for her to attempt to usurp Edward Heath's place in the referendum campaign in which he had always played the leading role and in a field which is likely to remain his greatest personal achievement. It would have been wrong, certainly, for her to adopt a purely combative stand against Wilson at a time when the country itself stands in so dire a peril.

Above With Michael Heseltine at a rally at Central Hall, Westminster, February 1975

Left Margaret Thatcher with Pierre Trudeau, Prime Minister of Canada

Above Mrs Thatcher with the US Secretary of State, Henry Kissinger

Right Madame Françoise Giroud, the French Minister for Women, and Margaret Thatcher, find something to amuse them at the opening of the Women and Power Conference in London in April 1975

bove Margaret Thatcher with Ronald
eagan, American ex-actor and ex-
enator

ght Mrs Thatcher at the Conservative
omen's Conference, May 1975

Right Mrs Thatcher has tea with the staff of the new Paris branch of Marks and Spencer, May 1975

Above Margaret Thatcher meets the French President, Valéry Giscard d'Estaing

ith William Whitelaw on the way to a meeting to boost the Tory campaign to keep Britain
the Common Market.

Above At the European Parliament with Peter Kirk *(right)*

Left Margaret Thatcher at the door of the show house at the Ideal Homes Exhibition, Olympia, March 1975

In Edinburgh during her 1975 tour of Scotland

Mrs Margaret Thatcher, after registering her vote in the Common Market Referendum, J
1975

What she must do is to win the confidence of the nation, and in this she has certainly been succeeding. As at the time when Lord Woolton and R A Butler rebuilt the party between 1945 and 1950, there is a real need to build up again a distinctive Conservative approach. Nationally there is a genuine necessity to give the country back confidence. Individually it is her task to give people back hope.

In March 1975 she made a major speech to the Federation of Conservative Students which is worth quoting in some detail, because it typifies her personal belief in the future.

'The more use you make of your opportunities in higher education, the better you do now and the more successful you look like becoming, the more threateningly will the forces of envy, restriction and egalitarianism be massed in your path.

'It is not just that the prospect of redistributive taxation will reduce your incentives and rewards, or that inflation will steadily erode your incomes.

'Whole areas of employment are changing in a way that makes the prospect of a satisfying career less likely.

'However strong his vocation, who is going to want to become a medical specialist or a hospital consultant in this country if the present trends continue?

'How many men or women of quality and independent mind are going to see a future for themselves in journalism, if Mr Foot and the militants of the NUJ and the printing unions have their way with the freedom of the press?

'How much excitement, or scope for enterprise and constructive effort, will young people see in an industry either controlled by Mr Benn or threatened—as now they all are—with nationalisation in the future?

'What certainty or continuity does entry into a family business or partnership offer, with taxation as it is now and the Capital Transfer Tax poised to demolish the undertaking in one or two generations? And what are the prospects if you try to start up on your own?

'If you feel a call to the public service, what chance will you have to plan wisely for the country's future or administer the system for the benefit of the people? You will be working to enforce narrow Socialist policies, increasingly concerned to stave off total disaster, increasingly reviled by taxpayers and ratepayers as an interfering bureaucrat or a spendthrift parasite?

'If your instinct is to fight back and to go on fighting for the right to a worthwhile life in a great country, you must help with the counter-attack.

'Because I shall never stop fighting. I mean this country to survive, to prosper and be free. And I need your help in the fight.

'I haven't fought the destructive forces of Socialism for more than twenty years in order to stop now, when the critical phase of the struggle is upon us.

G

'We shall revive hope for the future in the hearts of millions who have almost abandoned hope—and so revive and release their energies for the task of rebuilding Britain.

'We want you to be free to be yourselves and to make what you want of your lives. Not as servants of the state, but as partners in the common effort.

'We shall restore justice and common sense to the taxation system, so that it no longer inhibits enterprise and effort.

'We shall ensure that the taxpayers' money is wisely spent for the common good and for the benefit of the genuinely needy.

'We shall encourage and stimulate industry to create new wealth for the people of Britain.

'We shall, wherever possible, restore and encourage freedom of choice for the individual—in education, in housing, in shopping, in provision for the future.

'We shall ensure that Britain plays her full part in the development of Western Europe—in the defence effort of the Western Alliance.

'All this can be done, if enough people believe it can be done. There is such a thing as faith that can move mountains—although it requires a bit of planning and a bit of muscle as well.'

The British people are faced with a choice between two very different ways of life. Margaret Thatcher is determined that they should be free to make that choice, and she is equally determined that the future should not be lost by default.

10

'...Involvement is All-Important...'

'In politics,' said Ramsay Macdonald, 'you need to look not so much to the consequences as to the consequences of the consequences.'

In many ways British politics has been curiously without form over the last decade. There has been a large area of the middle ground that has found itself increasingly unhappy with the policies of each of the parties. Inflation, a disease which always eats at the guts of any country when it gets a serious hold, has put at risk many of the things which we have tended to regard as an automatic part of our way of life here: a stable society, an improving standard of living, the security of personal savings, an effective welfare state and a regular position of full employment. The fact that such fundamentals have been shown to be at risk has thrown the British people into a deep sense of uncertainty and gloom.

The political parties themselves have tended to change course with alarming rapidity. Labour, which in the early 1960s seemed set fair to emerge as a social democratic party ready to take its place as an effective alternative in the middle ground, has come increasingly under the influence of its left wing and now stands well to the left of most European Socialist parties. The Liberals, who have emerged from time to time as the beneficiaries of the other two parties' unpopularity, have been unable to persuade the electors, or even apparently themselves, that they have a coherent and effective solution. The Conservative Party has seemed to many people to have lost its identity and to have taken over the role of merely acting as a brake on increasingly extremist periods of Socialist government.

The emergence of Margaret Thatcher at this particular point in time is therefore of great importance. The qualities which she brings with her as a leader are ones which people in this country have felt to be largely missing in leadership during recent years. She has a fundamental philosophy which is based on clear and strongly held principles of her own. She is ready to look to the long-term future of the country. And she believes, with passionate dedication, that Britain has got a future based on freedom and individual choice, rooted in a mixed economy and not on a continual increase in state control.

There is little doubt that this is a view which many people, including some of those who have tended to vote Socialist, would share. If it was put to a free vote, like the referendum on our continued membership of the European Community, there would undoubtedly be an overwhelming majority in favour of keeping a free economy here and in favour of maintaining a balanced society of the kind on which we have long prided ourselves. The alarming thing, caused basically by the increase in the rate of inflation, is that many people have come to doubt whether any government can really put this into effect.

Margaret Thatcher believes that it can and must be done. For a start, she is essentially a moderate. No government, she argues, can be effective unless it has the support of the people as a whole. It can only operate effectively if it has got the people behind it. Public opinion has got to be generated to bring much greater pressure to achieve what it wants. It is, to her, a question of mobilising the cause of common sense.

This means that there must be an increasing dedication to the cause of open government. People do not want to feel that they are coming more and more under the yoke of a government which in turn becomes increasingly isolated from them except at election times. Power is a trust and therefore a responsibility but it cannot be operated without the maximum possible degree of consultation and involvement by those who hold it with those they hold it for.

One of the greatest achievements of John Wesley was that he restored the dignity of self-respect to millions of people whom the impersonal nature of the Industrial Revolution was tending to crush. 'Church or no church,' he argued, 'the people must be saved.' It was to this end that he believed that God had given man the fundamental gift of free will and therefore the fundamental gift of choice. This is the tradition in which Margaret Thatcher was brought up. Choice is a subject to which she reverts continually in her speeches and which lies very close to the basis of her political philosophy. If you take away from individuals the right of making their own decisions not only do they feel increasingly isolated but they become increasingly ineffective. We have a birthright of choice and this means that it is the job of a democracy to see that people have to the greatest possible degree the opportunity of exercising it. In the complexities of the modern world there is always an increasing undertow to put more and more of the process of decision making, in fields which affect the lives of individuals, into the hands of the politician or the bureaucrat. It is the task of the politician to fight this, to bring back the power to make decisions to the individual.

The connection between this and obtaining an effective government, which can achieve something for the nation, is to Margaret Thatcher an obvious one. If there is a freedom-loving, law-abiding majority in the country then it must be made to feel that the government is working for it. Confidence must be brought back, so that people feel a measure of trust in the quality of their savings, in the value of their money and in the future of their country.

First and foremost there must be an effective policy against the rise in the rate of inflation. This means that every valid measure must be operated towards keeping prices down. But as the last ten years have shown, there is no straight economic panacea to destroy this particular evil. It is only going to be overcome if the British people themselves will this to be done.

It is here, Margaret Thatcher has made clear, that the factor of involvement is all-important. It is no good people grumbling about what is happening in this country unless they feel that they have the power to do something about it. It is no good the silent majority complaining of what is happening to industry unless they are given the opportunity to control their own decisions. To this end she regards the principle of the secret ballot in union affairs and the opportunity for free voting during working hours as being fundamentals of industrial democracy.

But in her view it goes further and deeper than this. As she said in her speech to the CBI conference in 1974, the more that people working in any concern feel involved with its success the greater the chance is that a free economy will succeed. It is fundamental to human nature that people have got to feel part of the organisation for which they work, whether it is big or small. The worst feature that tended to develop in wide areas of industry and commerce during the nineteenth century was the feeling that the work force on which the prosperity of any organisation in the long run depended began to feel that they were cut off from playing a real part in its affairs. Strangely, this has tended to become even more true of the nationalised industries than it has of the private sector. Loyalty to a going concern is the vital factor but this is not going to exist unless employees feel that the board is just as much involved with their interests as it is with the shareholders, that they have a real role to play and an opportunity for development within any organisation and that their work is producing results for themselves and their families in the sense that they can save and build their own lives on the basis of the work of their hands or the work of their heads. If the prosperity of a firm is indivisible so must be the feeling of responsibility for it of everyone who works there. If they are giving their working lives to work for it, then they have got to be able to feel that it is their firm.

As the Soviet Union has effectively shown, the nationalisation of all the means of production, distribution and exchange, the fundamentalist Clause Four of the British Labour Party's philosophy, does not provide a long-term answer to this need. In a Marxist society the individual worker tends to become much more of a cog in the machine. The process of decision-making really does lie, more than ever, with unseen and unapproachable bureaucrats. In a mixed economy, in a free society, the measure of choice does remain. It is not a question of every decision being made by government. Control over government expenditure is untramelled in the one-party state. But can a free society continue to flourish in the west in a situation where the realities of power seem to be slipping more and more into the hands of a politically motivated minority?

It is Margaret Thatcher's case that it can. There has got to be a break to the increasing spiral of wage demands which cannot be supported by productivity and which put at risk the jobs of millions of other people throughout industry. If, as a recent government survey suggests, the average Briton in the 1970s is dissatisfied with his job, struggling to buy a house and maintain a car and a telephone and constrained by a battle to maintain his standard of living, then this is a trend that can and will be reversed.

As in so many other aspects of national life the problem comes back at root to inflation. Labour was elected in October 1974 on a programme of free collective bargaining. What this meant in terms was a blank cheque to the trade unions to print their own wage demands in key industries, irrespective of the implications for rising prices and increased unemployment. To the extreme Left this presented a developing opportunity that they could come to power through the chaos in which inflation might plunge the country.

It is doubtful whether there could be any one solution. Britain badly needed a social contract if this had meant more than a mere expression of pious and politically convenient euphemisms. In hard fact it has meant little or nothing. Cruellest of all is the assumption that is at present increasingly being expressed that we are not going to have the will to combat inflation until soaring unemployment figures of two million or more, with all the terms of human waste and misery that that represents, force us into doing so.

As the history of other Western European countries in recent years has shown, it is possible to contain the rate of increase. Government expenditure must be cut, more capital investment must be made available for industry. We have got to face the realities of funding our own expenditure by our own productivity of our exports and not by constant increases in high interest foreign borrowing. Put brutally, we have got to learn to cut our coat according to our cloth.

One of the important features about Margaret Thatcher in relation to this crisis is her determination to meet it in terms of her own distinctive Conservative philosophy. She has always believed in the value of savings, she has always fought against the belief that a country can achieve all its expectations by simply borrowing money and footing the bill as and when it can. She is pre-eminently a realist.

To this extent, I believe, she is sympathetic to the monetarist case which has been made in recent months by Sir Keith Joseph that we cannot just go on maintaining our expenditure by printing money, whatever the implications for our currency. It has been suggested that this represents a swing to the right, away from the principles of statutory wage and price control as operated by the Heath government and towards the free exercise of market forces. This is to misunderstand her basic stance. As a realist she is interested in the consequences of the consequences.

This means, I think, that she would be willing to use a combination of methods to fight the immediate crisis. She is certainly much too concerned with people to use a policy of deliberately allowing unemployment to achieve specific economic results. Equally, she is aware of the greater risk of creating much greater and more serious unemployment by failing to face up to the realities of the situation and temporarily buying a way out of trouble as Harold Wilson has done.

Her comments on government aid to firms in financial difficulty were very relevant to this. To keep down unemployment there was an acceptable case, she said, for government aid in these circumstances, but only where the firm concerned had got a valid future in the long term and it was not just a question of using taxpayers' money to sustain a position which could not validly be maintained. As a country, and as individuals, we have got to learn to stand on our own feet.

If Britain can come to live with the realities of this situation and to overcome the self-destructive tendencies within itself it could still be the most attractive country in the world in which to live. We have got a tradition of freedom and tolerance and of respect for the Rule of Law. We have built up for ourselves a long history of achievement in industry, particularly in the fields of engineering, science and technology. We have one of the most skilled work-forces in the world with a long tradition of craftsmanship, enterprise and adaptability. In such fields as banking, insurance, marketing and the arts we can still lead the world. This is the basis on which we can still build.

It is an intense awareness of this potential which is at the root of Margaret

Thatcher's determination that we should, despite everything that has recently happened, still succeed as a country. That the going is likely to be rough in the immediate coming period most people would now agree. The extent of our problems has led to a good deal of talk on the basis that the party system in British politics can no longer be effective. We should resign ourselves, it is argued, even to abandoning that element of choice and accept the need in the foreseeable future to being managed by a coalition.

Historically, this is a misunderstanding of the position. A war-time coalition has been a valid solution for a particular situation but in times of peace this has scarcely ever been successful. The Socialist Party is still too dominated by folk memories of Ramsay Macdonald to accept such a scheme. To break the basis of the party system would be to play into the hands of extremists either on the right or the left. The desperate urgency of our present problems calls for a solution, but not for solving by government by committee.

Margaret Thatcher's policy is to put forward a characteristically Conservative solution. Less than anybody is she under the illusion that the remedy is going to be an easy one. She is, as her past career has shown, a very determined woman and she has remarkable personal resources of energy and courage. At the height of the American depression it was President Roosevelt who struck new hope in the hearts of his fellow countrymen with the very simple message: 'We have nothing to fear but fear itself.' This is essentially what Margaret Thatcher hopes and is certain that she can do for Britain. The task of being the first woman Prime Minister in this country would not be an easy one in normal circumstances. Even a short time ago it would have been inconceivable. We have been fortunate, however, that the nation's desperate moments of crisis have generally produced for us leaders of special stature. If the British people are determined to overcome the crisis in which they now find themselves, if they share her belief that we have still got a great future, then in Margaret Thatcher they have found someone who could well turn the present doubts and fears into a period of real achievement.

11

We Want the Truth

Where does Margaret Thatcher stand in relation to the history of the Tory Party itself? Like her predecessor, she comes very obviously from outside the traditional pattern of the 'magic circle' and is therefore another healthy step away from the grouse-moor image of caricature. Equally her appointment is an indication of the kind of leadership that the party itself is looking for in the second half of the 1970s.

She has always herself regarded social mobility as being one of the great benefits not only of the British tradition as a whole but of the distinctive Conservative contribution to it. Labour has laid a great deal of stress in recent decades on class issues and on the rigid pursuit of equality. Conservatives instead have always preferred to stress the benefits which come from a varied pattern of society in which not everybody is, or wants to be, exactly similar. It is an important part of British life that someone in the position of Margaret Thatcher should be able to rise to the top job as she has. Equally, it is an important aspect that she should be able to do so as a woman.

Despite the satirical picture perpetuated by cartoonists Vicky and David Low, the tendency to choose their leaders from a wide social spectrum has always been a mark of the Tory Party, as Harold Macmillan, who himself, for example, was the grandson of a Scottish crofter whose son came to London and established himself in publishing, has said. Heath's father was a small builder in Thanet. Home and Eden came from orthodox upper-class backgrounds, Baldwin and Chamberlain from business origins in the West Midlands, Bonar Law was a Glasgow businessman who was born in Canada. The charge of Conservative premiers coming from a particular type of family simply does not hold water.

Perhaps the most unique figure among them all, Benjamin Disraeli, came from right outside the ordinary social circle of his time from which most of his Parliamentary colleagues, Conservative or Liberal, were drawn. The son of a Sephardic Jewish immigrant, he had neither the public school nor university education normal to his contemporaries in politics, and he began his parliamentary career against every sort of prejudice on account of the flamboyance of his appearance and career; he was yet the one man who did most to form the modern Conservative Party as we know it and who became the font of Conservative orthodoxy.

If it was Disraeli whose ideas dominated Conservative thinking until well into the present century, it was R A Butler whose influence was probably most important on the party's ideas between 1945 and 1970. Although he never became Prime Minister, Butler's effect as Chairman of the Party and as the guiding hand behind the Conservative Research Centre was to be enormously strong over the way in which Conservatism developed in the vital period after the war and following Sir Winston Churchill's electoral defeat in 1945.

By 1970 a new situation in the country was already coming into being. The influence of Butler's own Education Act of 1944, combined with the relative prosperity of the period of Macmillan's government, had produced an era in which openings for the young in particular and for those who wanted to work to build up a career on their own talents existed more than ever before. Wisely, the Conservative Party had maintained its facility to move with the times and had gained an image which enabled it to speak genuinely for a large cross-section of the community and for an extremely wide variety of interests.

The difficulty by the beginning of the 1970s was that the party had reached a stage when it was vital that a general re-think should be applied to a number of aspects of its philosophy. In opposition under Heath, between 1964 and 1970, detailed plans had been worked out in a considerable number of fields. These were, however, dependent on the success of Anthony Barber's policies as Chancellor of the Exchequer and on the prospect that an expanding economy would give the government the opportunity to implement many of the improvements to which it aspired. As both international and national events began to turn on Heath's Government, so he was left in a position where he found it increasingly difficult to decide in fact which way to go.

One major achievement will stand everlastingly to his credit—the entry into the European Economic Community. Other broad-based plans like Peter Walker's reform of local government, though successfully implemented in Parliament, contained the seeds of difficulties which were to trouble the new local authorities for some time to come and which had serious side effects in adding to the pressures on public spending. With hindsight, it was also unfortunate that the allied problem of rating reform was not dealt with at the same time.

The Selsdon Park Conference of Heath's Shadow Cabinet in January–February 1970, although it was felt to be generally right wing in feeling, dealt in essence with immediate solutions rather than basic principles. The proposals which emerged there concerned such issues as strengthening the police force and controlling threatening forms of demonstration, tightening controls on immigration, a policy for making agreements with trade unions legally binding and the reduction of direct taxation.

The question of industrial relations was one which was to trouble Heath's Government throughout its existence. During the Labour Government in April 1969 Harold Wilson had announced that he regarded the introduction of a bill to curb unconstitutional and unofficial strikes and create a more organised basis for relations in industry as vital to his Government's continued existence unless the TUC came forward with viable alternative proposals of their own. His decision in the end to back down on Barbara Castle's White Paper *In Place of Strife* was a substantial abdication of Wilson's own personal authority and that of his Government, with regard to their relationship with the trade unions and the left wing of the Labour Party.

Public opinion certainly expected Heath to act on this issue, particularly since it had played a considerable part in the Conservative manifesto in the 1970 election. In the event, when the Industrial Relations Bill was brought forward in Parliament by Robert Carr it was too prolix, too complicated and too difficult to enforce, although it contained provisions like the cooling-off period which, if it had been given half a chance, might have brought considerable benefits to industry. The passage of the bill in the House of Commons was stormy in the extreme. The emotion engendered in the country generally became very considerable. The position of the Industrial Court, which was set up when the Act was passed, became highly contentious and the way in which the Court was attacked as a political institution, quite unfairly to Sir John Donaldson, the distinguished Chairman, who approached his duties strictly as a High Court Judge, brought the position of the Law generally into controversy. The combative situation which attended both the passing of the Act and its subsequent application highlighted a situation which made the process of government in the country considerably more difficult. An added difficulty was that industry itself felt that it had been inadequately consulted on the preparation of the Industrial Relations Act and found substantial parts of it difficult to apply in effect.

Faced with the dual problem of rising unemployment figures and an increasing rate of inflation, Heath and Barber decided in the summer of 1971 to go 'hell for broke' for an annual increase of 5 per cent in overall production. A vast amount of government money was pumped into industry and John Davies's policy of plucking 'lame ducks' was reversed, without warning, by the application of specific sums of public aid to Upper Clyde Shipbuilding and the nationalisation of the aviation side of Rolls Royce, when both these fell into savage financial difficulties.

It was ironic that a Government which had begun its life by producing legislation to denationalise Thomas Cook's and the state pubs of Carlisle should shortly follow this by nationalising Rolls Royce. In the event of what was to come, the initial policy of winding up the government agencies concerned with consumer protection, the Industrial Reconstruction Corporation and the Prices and Incomes Board was to seem an additional irony.

Although the Heath Government did achieve its target of 5 per cent increase in production by the Spring of 1973 the economic and other difficulties in which it found itself not only severely limited its freedom of action but meant that no far-reaching attention was given to some of the major problems which were facing the country. These included the funding of the nationalised industries, the financing of the welfare State, the whole question of the way in which supplementary benefits were being paid out to strikers, particularly after a change in the law introduced by the previous Labour Government, and the question of money supply generally. In order to avoid immediate difficulties with regard to unemployment, at a time in 1971 when this stood at about 600,000 nationally, continuing extra amounts of money were pumped into circulation in the economy.

The far worse economic problems which have beset the Labour Government since have perhaps now at last persuaded the country as a whole of the need to come to grips with some of these problems before inflation itself brings unemployment to the two million mark. Denis Healey who, on one month's figures, was arguing in October 1974 that inflation was running at the rate of about 8 per cent nationally, has subsequently admitted that the effective rise by the summer of 1975 is approaching a level which threatens the whole basis of national economic stability and has pointed to the real risk of overpowering unemployment figures.

It is important from the point of view of Margaret Thatcher's relation with Conservative thinking generally that she has never belonged to what might be termed a clique of any kind within the party. She has always been inclined to judge issues much more from the basis of a general Conservative philosophy, which accords with her own strongly-held beliefs which have already been discussed, than been ready to see political answers as coming easily from any particular set of economic dogmas, however persuasive these might be. Two strands therefore are vital in regard to her approach to what course the party ought to take. One is to try to get it back to certain fundamentals of Conservative thinking from which she feels that the party has increasingly been swept away in recent years. The other is to take a broad general look at the problems of the present day and then apply basic principles in a practical fashion.

Like Disraeli, whose great strength it was, she is a whole-hearted believer in simplifying issues to their real essentials. Like him, she believes in the need for maintaining the really enduring parts of society and of rendering secure for the British people their inviolable rights. From her speeches, the Tory Party emerges again as being as it should be about very simple things.

Just as with the author of *Conningsby*, she is very much a politician of social conscience. Continually, throughout her career, she has shown herself aware of the duty of the community to protect those sections in it who tend, particularly in times of economic instability, to become the underdogs and to be overwhelmed by factors against which they do not have the ability to defend themselves.

This means that she is very much a believer in priorities and in the duty of society to exercise its real right of moral choice. Over the years the welfare state has become diluted by the decision to spread its benefits so widely, and often so unquestioningly, that the people whom it was intended primarily to benefit get less protection from it than they should.

Margaret Thatcher does not believe that it is the duty of the state to cosset and control the individual from the cradle to the grave. In matters of taxation and education, and of the provision of other services, she does not regard it as the place of government to establish an over-all control over the lives of people so as to enforce a standardised system of existence. She believes passionately in the right of individuals to decide how they are to live and work and whether they want to buy their own home. She believes passionately that the purpose of taxation is to provide society with enough money to run a compassionate, secure and effective form of government and not to impose on each of its members a way of life which restricts him to one particular view of how he ought to live.

It is too early, by far, to anticipate the terms of the Conservative manifesto at the next general election, on which she and her colleagues are now working and which will form the basis of her policies if she is elected. What it is possible to do is to predict the general form that this will take. In the main, I think, it will be a much simpler and more easily understandable document than has tended to be the case with most political programmes in recent years. She will ask, I believe, the British people to take a good look at themselves and at the kind of society in which they live and ask them to consider a number of fundamental questions.

Do they want to continue in a free society? Are they prepared to save and work for this? Do we acknowledge that we have a particular duty toward certain sectors of our society and, if so, are we prepared to use our resources to meet those responsibilities? Are we willing to show restraint in order to regain a basis of economic security without which life in this country has become increasingly uncertain and increasingly depressing for the vast mass of the population in recent years?

One of the reasons that people have tended to distrust politics to the extent they have over the last decade is that it is precisely these questions, which affect the basis of their lives, that have not been put fully enough to them at election times. Anyone who has been a Parliamentary candidate will be familar with certain and by no means infrequent types of reaction—'I don't care. What have any of them done for me?' 'They're all the same, all these politicians, only looking after themselves.' 'Look at them screeching at each other all the time on television. Why don't they do something for the country?' 'What's the use of my having worked hard all my life when every layabout can go down to the Labour Exchange and draw three times more than I've been able to save for without doing any work at all?' 'There's no difference between the parties anyhow. What can any of that lot do about the mess we're in?' 'I've given up voting since they gave Mrs Smith a constant attendance allowance for her Harry and they never did anything for me.'

And yet if the majority of these electors were asked what they wanted out of life, they would know very well what kind of life they did want and the majority would not opt for a state regimented existence. The failure of the Conservative Party in 1974 was that a lot of people who did not want socialism voted Liberal or Labour, or simply stayed away from the polls, because they did not understand what the Conservatives were about, because they wanted to take it out on the government for their existing difficulties or because they felt that a Conservative Government had ceased to take into account the basic matters with which they were concerned and therefore had not got a chance of getting things right for them.

Central to this problem is the continually increasing role of the state as the provider of all things. The more that the state itself has taken over parts of existence which used to be the responsibility of the individual or of groups of individuals within the community, the more the individual in turn becomes dependent upon the state. As this dependency grows so does a feeling of helplessness, lack of personal independence and irritation with the system. Once the government is established, either consciously or subliminally in people's minds as the universal provider, so there is likely to be an increasing annoyance when the cornucopia from which the goodies come does not prove to be a bottomless one. The example of Norton-Villiers-Triumph is a tragic case in point.

As her speech at Sheffield to the Conservative students showed, Margaret Thatcher is fundamentally concerned with what are the proper boundaries for the role of the state in a democracy. She is well aware that the overpoweringly centralised state can come in two ways. It can come by a direct take-over of the sort that we have seen recently in Portugal, where one undemocratic regime has merely taken over from another, or it can come from the constant drip, drip, drip of government interference in every facet of personal existence. She is, I think, more determined to concentrate on defining the limitations of state control than perhaps any other recent Conservative leader. She will certainly, as Prime Minister, be an insistent upholder of the position of Parliament as the elected and responsible body nationally, and of the rights of individual constituency members. In turn, she will be watchful of over-encroachment by the effects of delegated legislation.

One problem that she will have to face, and on which the Shadow Cabinet are working at the present time, is the vital one of how to finance the public sector of industry. While no one would deny the nationalised industries their share of achievement since 1945, the cost at which they have constantly had to be subsidised out of the taxpayers money has risen to near catastrophic heights. To a large extent this has not been the fault of the industries themselves but of governments, both Socialist and Conservative, who have constantly wavered over the provision which is made for their future. In the present situation the figures speak for themselves and present a staggering total amounting to a bill of close on £1,000 million a year for the taxpayer. The Gas Corporation losses announced in 1975 exceed £40 million, the Post Office approximately £300 million, the Electricity Council over £250 million and British Rail £349 million. The cost of a large part of these losses has been passed on to the consumer by way of increased charges for services. A large proportion of these increases resulted from substantial wage settlements.

When Harold Wilson dealt with the question of Britain's economic growth in an interview that he gave to *Time* magazine at the end of July 1975, he compared the position in this country with that in America. 'In the public sector,' he said, 'we have had a magnificent record of modernisation. Our railroads are so much better than yours are.' It is doubtful whether the last remark is altogether a fair comparison in any case between a small country where the railway system is still the basic network of communication and a very large one where air traffic and long distance buses also play an important part. What is really significant however is the failure here to define the point between where modernisation in the public sector is wholly necessary and will in due course pay for itself and where the need to carry such immense sums simply passes on to the public an additional but not inevitable burden which they cannot afford to pay. If we are not careful the nationalised industries are likely to remain an unwilling Trojan Horse in the fight against inflation. What, at any rate, has got to be done is to place these industries on such a footing that they know where they are as far as their borrowing powers are concerned and can plan their future accordingly.

It is indicative that, in the same interview with *Time* where Harold Wilson could speak proudly of modernisation in the nationalised industries, he accounted for the difference between economic growth in Britain and, for instance, in Germany and Japan by reason of inadequate investment in the private sector, and produced one of the oldest excuses in use, since the war, in the politician's repertoire. 'Germany, of course,' he remarked, 'had the advantage of the total destruction of their industrial equipment, while we were struggling with old looms, old machine tools and the rest.' This is perfectly true. But what is far more doubtful is his solution for this particular problem. 'Some of our new legislation is directly related to getting up the level of investment; for example, the National Enterprise Board will be intervening in one industry after another where investment has lagged.' What is vital here is to provide a position in which both private investment in industry and in turn industry's investment in its own capital equipment is established on a solid basis and that can only be done by an effective reform of the tax system. It is no use, as Margaret Thatcher has pointed out, taking vast sums out of industry by way of tax and then returning part of these on an arbitrary basis and with an increasing number of under-tones and strings attached. That is not the way that confidence is bred in industry.

The existence of a continuing threat of nationalisation to an unlimited number of private companies under a Labour Government does not tend towards confidence either. Continual surveys have shown that the majority of workers in private industry do not want to be transferred into public ownership but prefer to work as they are. What they do want is to be more closely identified with the companies for which they work and this is something which Margaret Thatcher has constantly stressed.

In the battle against inflation a further factor which has given rise to continual concern in the recent period is the constant increase in local authority spending. This is by no means entirely the local authorities' fault. Parliament has been far too inclined to lay duties on the councils, many of them admirable in themselves, without effectively costing what is involved. Although Margaret Thatcher is a firm believer in the independence of local government, it is clear from what she has said that the need for cut-backs in public expenditure will have to be a general one and that people, particularly those living on pensions or fixed incomes, who have budgeted on this basis, simply cannot afford to face constant substantial increases in the rates which they have to pay. It is part and parcel, in effect, of a single truth that she has repeatedly underlined. If we are to win against inflation we must only spend what we can afford.

It is a natural and understandable product of the reaction that has grown over central government in recent years that national patriotism and regional and local opinion within the United Kingdom has grown increasingly strong in the past decade. The issue has become a complicated one in that it has given rise to a pressure from some quarters for separate national states within the United Kingdom, which would lead not only to the dismemberment of Britain as we know it but would produce elements of scale in a Balkanisation of this country which would have totally unrealistic results. In the face of this, the study of devolution of powers which has been going on in the Shadow Cabinet under Margaret Thatcher's leadership is an acknowledgement of two very important principles which are extremely close to her own heart. The first of these is the right of people to have a say in their own affairs. The second is the need to recognise that people are different in different parts of the country and that these factors have to be taken into account. Although the majority of people in Scotland, for example, undoubtedly want to remain within the United Kingdom they also want it to be recognised that there is a Scottish identity and that Scottish interests need to be individually respected and fostered. The same thing applies to other parts of Britain.

What is intolerable is that the majority of important decisions, whether they may affect Scotland or, on a different level, affect East Anglia, should be made on a centralised basis and often with a minimum of local involvement. During her period at the Department of Education and Science, Margaret Thatcher was always extremely careful to involve local opinion when decisions had to be made involving any particular place or area, whenever she could. As she has said since, the most alarming thing that can happen under a Socialist Government is the extent to which it can go in crushing individual effort and suppressing individual initiative.

The fact that Margaret Thatcher herself comes from a provincial background and has sat for a number of years for a very varied suburban seat has certainly meant that she is widely aware of the necessity of taking a broad view of the problems and the needs of the country. Although it was predictable that such an attack would be made, as her subsequent actions since being leader have increasingly gone to show, nothing could be further from the truth than the suggestion that she would approach things with a South-eastern bias.

In a speech which she made in Northumberland on 31 July 1975, she stressed precisely the need to restore the opportunity for creating enterprise throughout the country. 'Ways have to be found,' she said, 'of releasing individual effort and making people feel that their enterprise is appreciated and that it is worth while making exertions and taking risks.

'The crisis that faces Britain should be taken as an opportunity to release precisely those talents and resources that have been locked up for too long. This may force the British people to look to themselves, using every ounce of inventive skill and individual enterprise.

'The Tory answer is, as Sir Winston Churchill defined it, to "set the people free". The Socialists are always talking about priorities but get them hopelessly wrong. They are so obsessed with the distribution of wealth that they forget it has to be created.'

In this same speech she spoke once again of the need for open government.

'We want the truth about unemployment. Today out of every thousand workers on Teesside, nearly one hundred have no jobs. There is 6 per cent unemployment on Wearside, nearly 7 per cent on Tyneside. We want to know the truth about wages. Is the Government really going to stand firm against the extremists? Or are we going to have special cases every time anyone challenges Mr Foot? We want to know the truth about government expenditure and, above all, we want the truth about the Government's intentions. We want no secret Bills, no private deals, but an open and honest policy to meet Britain's needs.'

She reiterated her basic plan to attack inflation on three fronts. There needs to be a steady and unflinching control of money supply to bring it down to a moderate rate of growth. The government's own spending, which has got totally out of control, must be cut hard. And there is a place for an incomes policy, not so much as a means of reducing inflation itself, but because its purpose is to reduce unemployment, its justification that if it is effective fewer people will lose their jobs.

The clear way in which she has spelt out this basic approach wholly gainsays Harold Wilson's assertion that a Tory Government would be committed to 'the monetarist heresy of using unemployment or financial policies that inevitably lead to unemployment' as their sole real means of dealing with inflation. Unless we are to reach the same sort of position regarding inflation as that in which countries like Iceland and Brazil now find themselves, control in future of the issue of money here must be adopted as a means of checking the long-term effects of inflation and in order to cut down large-scale unemployment rather than using unemployment as such as a weapon in the counter-inflationary battle.

Other countries, Margaret Thatcher pointed out, have taken steps to keep inflation in control and are now in a position to expand their economies again.

'We are not in a position to do that. The only thing Mr Wilson's Government did was to make inflation worse. They spent money recklessly and when it ran out they borrowed more.'

'Last February the Labour Government re-launched free collective bargaining as a product which would cure all our ills. Yet by October it was off the market, and its place was taken by a new product—the social contract. Now, nine months later, there is a new improved miracle, the £6-a-week Bill with the secret ingredient—so secret indeed, they haven't dared publish the formula. Mr Wilson has endorsed each new product with the assurance that it would save our country. So far two of their life-saving medicines have only made the patient worse.'

Margaret Thatcher herself is certainly unwilling to adopt any policy which might provide an easy but spurious answer. She has continually rejected the opportunity of putting forward any programme that might seem appealing to the electors but which has no basis in logical reality and which cannot be shown, to her satisfaction, to have an effective chance.

She has been pressed, from a number of quarters, to make an immediate commitment to the acceptance of proportional representation, both because it might be electorally popular and also because it could establish an effective common bridgehead with the Liberal Party. She has acknowledged that there is a need to consider Parliamentary reform. But, with typical honesty, she has also pointed to the realities of the present situation. This is not something which could be brought in before the next general election. It would mean a major change in our constitution and, before anything is done, there must be a Speaker's Conference, involving all the parties, so that the position can be fully discussed. The issues at stake, including an inevitable change in the system of constituencies and a break in the well-established method of each Member of Parliament being elected by and serving his own constituents, are too important to be judged arbitrarily and without being taken carefully into account.

Similarly she has refused throughout her career to buy votes by putting forward easy panaceas for social problems. She has always acknowledged the importance of housing in the life of the family. But she has stressed that the real way to meet the population's housing needs is not just to provide more and more council houses and cut back on the opportunities for growth in the private sector. As *The Times* put it, in a recent leading article, 'As a society we have been making progress towards being a property-owning democracy. We have now a choice between future development in that direction or development in a more explicitly Socialist direction, in which property is increasingly taken into the hands of the state. The biggest advance that could be made towards more equal distribution of wealth would be to give those who occupy council property the right to own it. This could put up the ownership of housing from 49 per cent to as much as 80 per cent. The objective of more widely spread wealth is surely the right one to adopt.' The words 'property-owning democracy' may be ones which have been around for a long time but the principle is one with which Margaret Thatcher would wholly agree.

In a speech which she made as shadow housing minister in the House of Commons in May 1974, she summarised her position:

'I agree that bad housing conditions are at the root of many of the problems in our society. It so happens that I had occasion the other day to turn out some election addresses. They went back to the first election I ever fought in 1950. I gathered together a clutch of election addresses written by people in my party and from the Labour Party. All of them said almost exactly what we are now saying about housing—namely that it is our objective to provide a decent home for every family. Some of the addresses are just as appropriate now as they were then. It is still an objective to provide a decent home for every family. That objective does not vary from one side of the House to the other.

'We know some of the problems of meeting that objective. We know, for example, of the problems of houses falling into decay faster than they can be replaced or renewed. We know some of the problems arising from the faster rate of household formation which means that we need more houses for the same number of people. However, our aims remain the same—namely to secure a decent home for every family. Progress will be adjudged by the progress that can be achieved, subject to the economic circumstances.

'In the Minister's (Anthony Crosland's) speech . . . we have central control, direction, nationalisation and municipalisation. There is the whole lot, one after another. I took the phrases out of the right honourable gentleman's outline of (housing) policy and put them together. . . . The truth is that the right honourable gentleman welcomes the power of compulsion. He likes central direction. The Socialists immediately think of solving a problem by the Government taking power and property and keeping it, and not by helping people to solve the problem by themselves and then handing back property.

'In the United Kingdom we have a higher level of council housing, I believe, than anywhere in Europe. Council housing already represents 30 per cent of all housing. Many of us take the view that while there are reasons from time to time for a local authority to purchase houses from the private sector, there are no compelling reasons for an authority to retain them or to continue to increase the number of houses under its control. I hope that authorities will not retain such houses, thereby getting an ever-increasing proportion of the total housing stock. I do not believe that this would be good for some of the housing areas or good for the country as a whole.'

In relation to the Welfare State, she has stressed three things. It must be made as effective as possible and based on satisfactory and effective financial provisions. There must be a continued place for the voluntary spirit and for the voluntary service within the community as a whole. The primary aim of the welfare services must be to ensure that people who really need help get it and not to provide a formalistic across-the-board service if this falls down on its basic duty of care because the services made available become either too indeterminate, too detached from the individual or too expensive to enable proper provision.

Uniformity is the major threat to individualism in the modern world. The Conservatives have always believed that the individual is more important than the state, when it comes to the long run, and that the family is a more important unit in the community than the neighbourhood centre, however useful some of these may be. It is because Margaret Thatcher has gone back precisely to these Conservative roots and has made them the centre of her political belief that she is so credible and hopeful a figure for all those who do not believe in Socialism.

12

It's Time Mrs Thatcher Had Her Chance

How have people in Britain reacted to Margaret Thatcher as a political leader?

As we have already seen she has been receiving a tremendous reception wherever she has gone so far in all parts of the country. She has already generated enormous indications of enthusiasm and affection. What have individual reactions been like?

Most people are certainly very interested in her. The majority of them were totally surprised when she emerged as the Conservative leader because they knew comparatively little about her and because they had not reckoned on a woman in this particular position. There was in fact a candidate who fought the election in October 1974 as an *Independent Conservative Margaret Thatcher for a Woman Prime Minister* in one seat, but he was certainly only an advance guard of what was to happen later.

People have got used remarkably quickly to a woman in the job. When she was first elected there was inevitably some degree of open-mouthed reaction. What would the members of the Carlton Club, that bastion of male Conservatism for over a century, do, for instance, about having a woman in their midst, since the leader of the Tory Party is automatically an *ex officio* full member? The Carlton Club in fact immediately coopted her, showed themselves to be delighted with their new addition and have proudly hung in one of their principal rooms the original of a Giles cartoon published soon after her election which was presented to them by Lord Wolverton. This shows a number of senior members of the club watching the installation of a Tannoy system there with some anticipation while one of their number is saying, 'It's going too far if she's going to have mass renderings of Jerusalem by a Women's Institute Choir here all the time.'

On a more serious level, some sections of the press did not know what to make of her either. There was a tendency to concentrate in certain papers on what, to adopt Doctor Johnson's celebrated phrase, might be termed 'the remarkable thing is that she is doing it at all' aspect of the case rather than on what Margaret Thatcher actually stood for.

Others fell into the trap of regarding her as a sort of stereotyped, blue-hatted, Conservative conference kind of lady and sought to typecast her accordingly. It is interesting that this sort of mistake was made much more by the general run of Fleet Street rather than the specialised lobby correspondents who worked at Westminster and already had some knowledge of Margaret Thatcher's warmth and strength of character. Certainly, remarks about her 'Dresden China prettiness' and about her seeming 'a typical bazaar-opening Tory female' have been much less frequent since the press as a whole have got to know her better. She has had an immense amount of newspaper coverage since her adoption but by far the greatest part of this has been concerned with her ideas and what she stands for rather than with trivialities.

Shirley Williams, herself a leading woman politician, has put her finger on something a good many people are thinking in an interview with Milton Shulman of the *Evening Standard*. 'A Parliament with more women in it would bring a more workaday attitude to the debates and more closely reflect the interests of all the people. It is not true that in argument women are intuitive and men logical. Mrs Thatcher, for example, reasons much more logically than Sir Keith Joseph or Enoch Powell, whose views are guided by intuitive feelings.'

It would be fair to add that Margaret Thatcher's speeches are a good deal more closely and logically reasoned than those of Mrs Williams's own leader, Harold Wilson, and do not have the tendency to folksy emotion that has become a part of Wilson's armoury when he is arguing a difficult case.

The frankness and clearness with which she speaks has brought back an element in discussion which has been increasingly missing in British politics in recent years. A number of people, some of whom voted against him, now acknowledge that Edward Heath was speaking a very considerable degree of the truth when he warned the country of the dangers which it faced in 1974. Although he had devoted adherents, many others among those who at present accept that he was right after all could not identify with him. They can and do identify with Margaret Thatcher.

The voters can also identify with Harold Wilson but they have found it increasingly difficult to do so since the failure of the social contract and since an increasing number of them have felt that his attitude in the October 1974 election in particular bore no relationship to the real gravity of the national problem as in fact it is. Wilson is a politician who has an answer for everything. The danger lies, in terms of his own political credibility, when the assertive nature of his own particular brand of confidence is seen to be backed by a very much less rose-coloured reality.

Ordinary voters have come, in a short period of time, to value two things in particular about Margaret Thatcher. One is that she does not mince words. The other is that she uses language that they can understand.

Shirley Williams's view that women on the whole are logical rather than intuitive in their approach to politics is one which is shared by a good many other women. Many women certainly feel an element of relief that we have at last got a woman in a position to influence what is happening. This view was forthrightly, if amusingly, put by a teenager, called Jean Laidlaw, from Leeds, who wrote to the *Daily Mail* recently. 'I think we are getting closer to having a woman Prime Minister and I think it's about time. I find that girls are much brighter than boys. It's time Mrs Thatcher had her chance. Some of the boys in my class don't even know the difference between Labour and Conservative theory. Heaven help them when they grow up!'

In terms of how a good many people feel about her it is an important fact that she is a comparatively new face in the centre of the political arena. It is also relevant that she is a woman. A good many Socialists very much regret the fact that they did not get in first with Shirley Williams and that her position is too moderate ever to make her acceptable to forces in the Labour left who have considerable power as the party is at present constituted.

But it is in Margaret Thatcher herself, irrespective of anything in the background, that the voters are really interested. They have certainly been watching her with a good deal of attention over the months since she became Leader of the Conservative Party. While the credibility of the Labour Government under Wilson has become increasingly wobbly, public respect for her has gone up. At the same time other political reputations have been decidedly on the wane. It is a measure of Margaret Thatcher's own success that no one concerned with the future of the Tory Party could regard Enoch Powell even as a remote rival to her, while under Edward Heath he remained a very definite possible contender. Jeremy Thorpe and the Liberals, though they remain potential vote-splitters among the anti-Socialists, have disappeared more and more into a present position of insignificance. And Anthony Wedgwood Benn's career, despite the ideological overtones, has taken harm in the public viewpoint through his involvement with disastrous mistakes over Court Line and the British motor-cycle industry.

Each of those made mistakes that Margaret Thatcher is not likely to make, Powell by involvement with extreme right-wing intransigence, Thorpe by the adoption of electoral gimmickry, like his hovercraft assault on the beaches, and Benn by the cultivation of a whizz-kid image that has let him down in the outcome. But it is interesting to compare her career with each of these for a number of reasons. Of the three of them, Benn is by far the most significant political figure but he has shifted his ideological base continually to the left while Margaret Thatcher has retained the same political stance in essence throughout the whole of her career. Powell, despite all his gifts as an intellectual and a speaker, has allowed himself to become totally divorced from the centre ground in a way which Margaret Thatcher, who has a natural tendency towards modera-tion, never could. Thorpe, in spite of his considerable personal charm and flair, has allowed himself to fall into a typecast role as the patron of the protest vote and is increasingly unable, as time goes on, to persuade the electors either that he stands for a united party or that he is a politician whom they can take wholly seriously and can trust to put a strong policy into effect.

Margaret Thatcher is a wholly serious politician and this is something that people like about her. Individuals can take politics seriously for a number of different reasons and in a number of different ways. They can be swayed by personal ambition, they can be influenced by a desire to impose their own ideological opinions on others, they can feel that they have a mission to achieve some particular end. Just as there are many reasons that bring people into politics so there are a good number that bring them to want to play a leading part in it. In Margaret Thatcher's case people do feel that she is fighting for something in which she passionately believes and admire her for doing so.

There are some people, of course, who do not like her as a political leader just because she is a woman. After so many years there is bound to be a certain degree of resistance simply to the idea of a potential woman Prime Minister. Some people resent the ease with which she appeared to come to the job, forgetting the long years of apprenticeship. Some people say that they dislike her for having too clear-cut a personality, for presenting too smart an appearance, for speaking with too 'plummy' a voice. Certain Conservatives cannot forgive her for having succeeded Ted Heath, though they forget the ease with which the latter took over from Sir Alec Douglas-Home. Certain Socialists cannot forgive her for being there at all.

But when the list of those who are violently opposed to Margaret Thatcher is added up it is evident that a far higher proportion of people, even among her opponents, tend to like her as a personality than is normally the case among top politicians. Certainly, a far higher proportion of people tend to feel an active enthusiasm for her than has been the case with a political leader for very many years.

What sort of feelings do people have about her potential performance in office? There are some who doubt a woman's capacity to control effectively a cabinet predominantly composed of men. Her success both with the formation and operation of her shadow Cabinet has already shown this to be nonsense. Others have claimed that a woman, particularly one in middle age, is not up to the physical and emotional strain of making frequent and important decisions or coping with the sheer volume of work in the way that a man could. As Shirley Williams replied when the same point was put to her by Milton Shulman: 'It is all really a matter of temperament.' Some men, in fact, can get, despite all appearances of robustness, unexpectedly wrought up under pressure. Women are frequently constitutionally capable of reacting to any situation in a calm and well-organised way.

Apart from the question of making the eventual decision, which must frequently lie with a Prime Minister or a party Leader, there is also the factor of being able to delegate. Here there is very much a plus mark for Margaret Thatcher. Unlike Wilson, she is capable, once she has studied a matter, of coming to a firm decision fairly quickly. Unlike Heath, but like both Attlee and Macmillan, she is capable of effectively delegating responsibility to her colleagues and then not interfering with them once this has been done.

She is not quick to promise things that she may not be able to do and when she does undertake to do something then she makes it a question of priority to keep her word. Politically in some senses this may make her a more rigid politician than certain others, but the electors are already beginning to sense that they are dealing with a political leader who means what she says and who does not hesitate to speak out.

If she has a fault as party leader at the present, it is perhaps a tendency to try to cover too much ground. Her private office is generally full of people waiting to see her, and she has only a comparatively small staff to cope with things. In addition to long and extremely exhausting tours in all parts of the country, she has taken on visits behind the Iron Curtain and to America for autumn 1975. In the meanwhile she has encouraged her own political supporters to be ready for an election which may come well before it would normally be expected.

Obviously, visits of this kind abroad are vital for a top level international political figure and Margaret Thatcher will have to continue to undertake them in addition to her existing duties in this country. The amazing thing is that she has got the physique and the stamina to carry this off, just as she managed to do as much as she did in her days as a candidate at Dartford or as a minister with a family to look after.

Although she has been round the country a great deal since February 1975 she has been wise not to rush in too much in terms of over-exposure on television. During the period that he was Prime Minister, Edward Heath tended to appear on television too little, possibly because he never felt entirely at home in the medium. Harold Wilson senses rightly that he is good at it but tends to appear on it too much. Margaret Thatcher had had to find a happy medium and has been successful with this, so that viewers did not switch off her Party Political Broadcast in the way that they usually do those of most politicians.

She gets an immense mail as a result of her speeches and her appearances on television, and it is always carefully and methodically dealt with. She answers a surprising number of letters in her own handwriting.

One major risk so far as the Conservatives are concerned has been averted by the choice of their new leader. In October 1974, as a result of the election, it really did seem possible that the party's reverses could reduce it in effect to a southern orientated party and one which predominantly represented agricultural seats. Now, the effect of Margaret Thatcher has been to restore both the morale of the party in the industrial seats and the general feeling that the party has recovered its cohesion as a whole. It is an important part of Margaret Thatcher's appeal that she can speak for people on as wide a basis as possible. As she herself said in her speech to the 1922 Committee at the close of the Summer session, after her first six months of leadership, Conservative policy needs to be simply and clearly stated so that people can understand how basic this is and how closely rooted on the dual principles of individual ownership and personal responsibility.

What the electors have welcomed, wherever she has spoken, has been the insistence that there is a fundamental difference between the Conservatives and their opponents. The more that the Labour Party lurches towards the left, the more important it is that the Tory Party should speak with an absolutely clear voice.

Much, much more than the Labour Party, Margaret Thatcher is determined that this country should be based on a good social mix. She has regularly rejected the Socialist view on egalitarianism because she regards this as thoroughly fraudulent. She has been, and is, totally opposed to the concept of the grey state in which the majority of the population would live on identical incomes in increasing dependence on central authority while a small elitist minority has the power to tell everyone else how to run their lives.

To understand the depth of Margaret Thatcher's repugnance against this element of contemporary Socialism it is necessary to understand the circumstances in which she first gained her political experience. Although in the history books, the Labour Government of 1945–51 will go down as a comparatively moderate one, it coincided with a period, immediately after the war, which gave it the possibility of wielding a quite frightening amount of power, with the continuation of rationing of every sort, control over the availability of materials for industry and commerce, fixed travel allowances, and direction of labour. It was the age of the first overwhelming increase in bureaucratic power in this country, a period in which 1984 was conceived by George Orwell, and it gave a very salutary lesson to anyone who was concerned with the freedom of the individual.

A good many people today have forgotten this period of austerity and restriction or are too young to remember it. They have even forgotten that it was this period that caused Sir Winston Churchill to coin his celebrated phrase that he would 'set the people free'. Margaret Thatcher was at Oxford when the first post-war Socialist government began, she had already been a candidate at Dartford twice by the time that it ended. She has the clearest reasons for remembering what happened then. She also has the clearest of reasons for reminding people now what, given the powers once again that were dismantled in 1950, a Labour government could now prove to be like if given its head. The difference between the then Labour Government and one now, however, would be the difference between the social democrat moderation of the Attlee Government and the kind of Marxist society envisaged in Stuart Holland's *The Socialist Challenge*.

Margaret Thatcher's great battle so far has been to persuade the electors that there is just such a fundamental difference between the two parties and between the two ways of life. She has also had to convince people that Conservatism is a positive creed. Both of these objectives she appears to have been achieving with increasing success in recent months.

Because of the increased realisation of the urgency and magnitude of the problems with which we are faced it is probably fair to say that people are more inclined to listen to her in any case than they were to Edward Heath. But it is also because she has set about the basic problem of communication in an entirely different way.

She has spent less time than he did, in opposition, in direct confrontation with the other side, either in Parliament or in the country. She has been criticised for this and it must be painful, for example, for somebody who enjoys the cut-and-thrust of argument as much as she does, not to take every opportunity to pursue it. But it was fundamentally a right decision. It is for her colleagues like Michael

Heseltine and Eldon Griffiths to pursue the individual mistakes made by Wedgwood Benn and other Socialist ministers. Margaret Thatcher's job, as Leader, has been to probe the Government as to what their intentions and their policies are, to make herself responsible for Conservative policy as an effective alternative and to make sure that this is put forward with maximum possible impact.

It is clear that on present showing, if there was to be an election in the immediate future, Margaret Thatcher would be returned by a very large majority. In one sense, purely taken as a result, this would be neither here nor there. When Harold Wilson won the election in February 1974 by the smallest of recognisable margins he could hardly have been said to have carried with him a substantial majority of the electorate. The last thing in the world that Margaret Thatcher would want, under present circumstances, would be to become his successor on a similar basis.

One has got to differentiate, therefore, as far as her effective prospects are concerned, between the possibility of another short-term negative result in favour of the principal opposition party and the alternative of a genuine decision in her favour on the real issues that are at stake. It may well be that in such circumstances a result can be narrow—for example, Sir Winston Churchill's victory in 1951 and Harold Wilson's in 1964 were narrow in the extreme but at any rate they were clear results. What Margaret Thatcher and the Conservatives have got to look for this time is an election result which not only gives them an overall majority but which shows a clear mandate against the way that politics in this country have been sliding towards the left and which shows a definite decision for a free market economy.

The chances are, increasingly, that she will get such a decision. The inference from talking to people of all sorts of political opinions seems to be that they realise just how important the next election will be and just how crucial the issues involved are.

It is easier perhaps for Margaret Thatcher to put these issues in their real terms than it would be for any other non-Socialist politician. If one looks at the runners-up to her in the second election for the Tory leadership, able as each of these was, one begins to realise just how great the change has been over the last few months. If one talks to people in different parts of the country, there is a degree of certainty this time about the Conservative leadership that has not really existed for a considerable period.

It has been interesting to talk to people on just this basis. In the recent past there has been an undoubted degree of resistance to politics, whatever the circumstances. People have been unwilling to talk about how they felt, unwilling to commit themselves, even if they were prepared to say that they did not accept the idea of a Socialist millennium. In the months since her victory, the atmosphere has changed very much. Not only are a far larger number of them prepared to come out into the middle and say how they feel, but there is a far more definite expression of opinion in favour of Margaret Thatcher's conception of Conservatism than there has been for most recent Conservative governments.

Partly, of course, this is because the voters have come to feel a total degree of disillusion with the Labour Party and what it stands for. Partly it is because they feel that there is a Conservative leader who expresses a broad consensus of what they themselves are concerned with. But, to a very considerable degree, it is because Margaret Thatcher has been able to establish herself as somebody whom the bulk of the population feel they can trust, because she has been able to express an attitude to politics that many people can themselves sympathise with.

It would be wrong to overemphasise yet the change in opinion that has taken place. Politicians as a whole are still subject to a considerable degree of distrust. Voters still obviously feel both a great deal of gloom about the system and a great deal of uncertainty about the future. But there has been a breakthrough. There is a real difference today between the number of people who say that they would vote for Margaret Thatcher because they regard this as the lesser of two evils and the number who feel that in voting for her there is a real chance of being able to achieve the kind of society that they want. Harold Wilson has a lot of obvious practical advantages, even at this stage in political development. He can call the date of a general election. He can rally his own side by underlining the implications that such an election would involve. He can slant his policies towards winning such an election when it takes place.

What he cannot do is shift Margaret Thatcher on the basic ground of what such an election will be about. She may not be the most subtle politician who has led the Conservative Party in recent years. She may not be the most intellectual. In terms of political technique she has nothing like the experience that Wilson himself has. What she has got, and what people feel about her, is an ability to put her case to the most effective degree and with complete honesty. Neither her own party nor the country as a whole could ask for more.

13

A Woman at the Top

How will a woman cope with being Prime Minister and with all the responsibilities that go with the job? Is a female premier likely to be very different in effect from the long succession of men who have previously held the office? These are questions that a good many people have been asking themselves in recent months as a result of Margaret Thatcher's success in the leadership election.

Even a matter of a few years ago it would have appeared inconceivable that a woman would be leading one of the two major parties in this country in the middle of the 1970s. Now, it seems increasingly probable in fact that Margaret Thatcher will be the next Prime Minister. Why has the climate of opinion changed to such an extent and what does this change portend?

It is 56 years since Lady Astor first took her seat in the House of Commons and Sir Winston Churchill said that he felt as if she had walked into his bathroom when he was in the bath and had nothing to protect himself with except his sponge. Since then there have been a number of extremely able women Members of Parliament, some of whom have risen to senior ministerial office. Prime Ministers have come to accept it as axiomatic in recent years that there should be at least one female member of their cabinet. Several of these, including Margaret Thatcher herself, have had considerable influence in the positions that they have held. Is a woman in the top job itself likely to lead to a substantial change of emphasis or to a new style of government?

One of the people who has given a good deal of thought to the role of women in politics is Françoise Giroud, a member of President Giscard d'Estaing's cabinet and the first ever Minister for the Condition of Women. In her recently published book *I Give You My Word*, she has come to a number of conclusions which are

127

both interesting in themselves and very illuminating in the case of Margaret Thatcher.

'In order to qualify in men's minds,' she writes, 'one has to be attractive, successful in a profession and have children. If men were asked to have all these virtues before they were qualified to speak up, how many would one find?'

All the pre-conditions that she states in fact apply to the present leader of the Tory Party. But she goes on to consider something which is much more important with regard to the way that the feminine mind approaches politics.

'I can't be duped by power,' Françoise Giroud states. 'I think only men can be. Women know that power in itself cannot give them the essential things in life. It is just an ersatz.'

This is an attitude with which, I think, Margaret Thatcher would thoroughly agree. Just as she said, at her first press conference as leader, that men were too fond of long, waffly answers to political questions, so she is inclined to feel that they are over-concerned with the details and the trappings of political life, rather than with the job of getting things done. Women are concerned, in Françoise Giroud's words, with the essential things of life and they have a capacity for getting down to fundamentals and a preference for being involved with results rather than for laying emphasis purely on broad strategy.

This does not mean that Margaret Thatcher herself is not concerned with basic principles. If anything, her views on matters of principle have tended to be a good deal more fundamental than those of a good number of her Conservative colleagues. What it does mean is that she has got an immediate capacity for mixing principle with reality.

It has sometimes been said that the government which could do most for this country would be one which was willing to impose on itself a self-denying ordinance about bringing in new legislation during its period of office and thus to concentrate on essentials. To some extent this is a counsel of perfection. Governments have to govern, to bring in finance bills to meet the nation's economic problems and to deal with the new issues which continually arise and need legislative action. Nevertheless, there is a germ of truth in it. We are overburdened with legislation today just as we are overburdened with taxation, and there is a real and vital need to get back to essentials.

This is where the place of Margaret Thatcher as a potential woman Prime Minister is important. She has been disinclined, and has been criticised for this, to tie her hands too firmly since taking over the leadership of the Conservative Party by committing herself to hard and fast policies in the economic field. Criticism on this issue has been applied to the fact that while she has been ready to state her belief on general principles she has been unwilling to tie the Conservative Party to specific economic remedies of a detailed kind before taking office. One of her most intelligent and sympathetic critics, Patrick Cosgrave, the political editor of *The Spectator*, has regretted that she was not prepared to undertake an immediate root and branch onslaught on Harold Wilson's anti-inflationary proposals, on the grounds that these constitute a phoney package, even if it meant precipitating an immediate general election.

As a woman leader it is probably one of her greatest gifts that she has been prepared so far to keep a comparatively low profile in matters of detailed policy while never wavering on issues of principle. As she herself said, 'There is much to do. I hope that you will allow me to do it thoughtfully and well.' In an age of instant politics and constant exposure to the media, this has caused some disappointment, particularly among political pundits. But what is important is that, just as she has returned continually in her speeches to the principles of freedom of choice and of the individual's right to make his or her own decisions, so she has stood four-square on her belief in a free economy. Capitalism has not necessarily been over-fortunate in its philosophical protagonists in this country in recent years, and Margaret Thatcher's defence of the free economy has been vital because she has made it clear that she supports it not on oblique partisan grounds but because she believes fully that it is the only system that can give the people of this country as a whole effective benefits and opportunities.

Sir Isaiah Berlin once wrote an intriguing critique of Tolstoy's philosophy called *The Hedgehog and the Fox*. In it he defines the great novelist's distinction of human beings into two principal types of personality, the hedgehog who has one big aim and works carefully and consistently to achieve it, and the fox, who rushes about all over the place trying to establish a number of different aims and generally producing less in the result.

If one accepts this definition, then intelligent women on the whole probably fall into the category of the hedgehog rather than that of the fox. They tend to know what they want to achieve in overall terms and set their minds to doing this. The theme of getting things done, from a practical point of view, is one to which Margaret Thatcher has returned over and over again both in her career as a minister and in her pronouncements as a party leader.

It is interesting, in this light, to compare her with recent Prime Ministers and their styles of government. The one which she will probably most resemble is Harold Macmillan, for whom she has a high regard. Macmillan was by no means a typical Tory leader, but he caught the imagination of people and their confidence in a way that few other post-war premiers have achieved, and his period of office from 1956 to 1964 is now looked back on as one of considerable achievement. His views had been forged to a great extent not only by his personal

I

service in the trenches in the First World War but also by his subsequent experiences as a young Member of Parliament for the highly industrial seat of Stockton-on-Tees during the Depression. What he also learnt during the extended period in which he was by no means in favour with the establishment of his party, up to the Second World War, was the importance of maintaining an effective course with which the majority of people in Britain could not only themselves identify but in which they understood the aims for which his government was working.

Like all other political leaders, Macmillan made mistakes but he succeeded in steering the country, at a time when our international position was inevitably on the wane and we were already threatened by the effects of inflation, into a position which not only gave us an honourable role in world affairs but managed to maintain an economic balance which provided for an effective degree of material prosperity and a marked sense of social responsibility in the face of an already existing tendency for spiralling wage demands. It is said that he wrote out in his own hand a quotation from *The Gondoliers* which was circulated among all the staff at 10 Downing Street: 'Quiet, calm deliberation disentangles every knot.' He managed, in any case, to achieve in British politics a degree of calm and of reality, against a difficult background, which has hardly been equalled in recent years.

Sir Alec Douglas-Home's brief period of office was probably too short for effective comparison with his successors, though he went on to become, as Foreign Secretary, a statesman of world class.

Harold Wilson, who has been referred to by one of his own biographers as the 'pragmatic premier', is probably the epitome of Tolstoy's conception of the fox. One of the truest remarks which he ever made was the often quoted one that a week in politics is a very long time. There is a difference, however, between pure pragmatism and a sense of political realism and this is a major distinction between him and Margaret Thatcher. He has proved himself in many ways an extremely accomplished tactician, but he has repeatedly failed to distinguish in government between the short-term advantages of tactics and the long-term benefits of any form of effective strategy. As a result he has become obsessed with the need to maintain, irrespective of the long-term issues, a balance in his own party and has presided over a slide into hyper-inflation and into an unrealistic domination from the left.

Edward Heath started, like Margaret Thatcher, with the advantage of coming from outside the magic circle of Tory politics, a position which gave him great potential importance in a society which was changing rapidly but was still unwilling to accept the inevitable and unsympathetic consequences of dogmatic Socialism. Like his successor, he was motivated by a strong sense of patriotism and few governments have been more motivated with a moving sense of purpose than was his administration in 1970 when he proclaimed his determination to bury the destructive effects of 'the two nations' in this country. Unhappily he lacked to a marked degree the ability to communicate with the people on whose behalf he was governing. When his government was blown off course, as it was by events which were not entirely under his own control, although he was right in much that he said and stood for, he was unable to put over to a great many people the vital nature of the stand that he was making.

Because of a certain similarity in their origins and background, the left-wing press was quick to claim that in choosing Margaret Thatcher the Conservative Party had moved on to a female counterpart of Edward Heath. 'The Conservatives have simply gone out of the frying-pan into the fire,' one leading Socialist commentator claimed. 'There is nothing to choose between either of their leaders.'

In fact, as recent events have proved, the differences between them are profound in many ways. As Prime Minister, Edward Heath was essentially a loner who preferred to govern on his own or with the advice of a small group of his closest colleagues. He found it difficult to take the views of his back-benchers, although he tried hard to do so, and they in turn found it difficult to communicate with him. To the public he gave, in the end, an abrasive and resistant impression, which belied the truth of his very real desire to reach an honourable settlement, particularly with the unions. When the U-turns began to take place, the Conservative Party as a whole were left feeling that they had not really been consulted and did not know precisely where their Government was going. In many ways this was a tragic development, since he was and remains a man of many qualities.

Margaret Thatcher is provided with many capacities which Heath does not have. She is a good listener, is sensitive to the opinions of others and she has a real ability to seek advice and, where she is persuaded that it is right, to act upon it. She is not only aware of the need to communicate the reasons for decisions to the public but has got the ability to do this. Her ordinary contact with people is easier than Heath's. One of his difficulties, as Prime Minister or as party leader, was that many people tended to find him a cold figure politically, partly because of the rather rigid nature of his television appearances, until they heard him speak in the flesh or met him personally, when they were frequently won over to him.

Apart from the effective style of her public appearances Margaret Thatcher has an outgoing personality which puts people at their ease quickly. On the day of the recent England–Scotland soccer international at Wembley, she was shopping in Sloane Square. Scots in their thousands had poured into London for the game and a large group of them were seeing the sights and recognised her. 'Look,' the cry went up, 'there's the leader of the Tory Party!' She immediately went over and shook hands and chatted and the encounter ended up with the visitors, who must have included a fair proportion of her political opponents, banging her warmly on the back, wishing her good luck and giving her a resounding cheer, to the complete surprise of passers-by. Although Ted Heath could be extremely pleasant when he talked to people individually, this was a far cry from the sort of impression that he gave, for instance, when his car was held up for some time in London traffic and he telephoned Sir Desmond Plummer, the leader of the GLC, who was on an official visit to Japan, to complain about the state of rush-hour traffic with which most Londoners were anyway only too familiar from continual experience.

As a woman, Margaret Thatcher is very well aware how much small problems mean in people's lives. But she is also well aware of what the major problem of inflation means to most families. Since this will be the major problem that her government will have to face, it is important that she feels as passionately about this issue as she does. Harold Wilson has, to a considerable degree, been fighting the rise of inflation with one hand tied behind his back since, having put forward the social contract as a general panacea, he was bound by the willingness of individual union leaders and his own left-wing Members of Parliament to support a policy of restraint. When he proposed, months later, the application of a £6 maximum increase, nothing showed up more clearly the fundamental unreality of his position than his unwillingness to disclose, under questioning by Margaret Thatcher, what statutory sanctions he had in mind to enforce his new programme.

As a lawyer, she is very well aware that it is no use having laws unless these are effective and the great majority of the public is determined to see that the law is imposed. In her recent speeches she has turned continually to this theme. The importance of the attitude of the Labour majority in Parliament to the issue of allowing the Clay Cross councillors to get away with openly breaking the law, and of the vehement participation of many Labour members in support of the Shrewsbury pickets who were convicted for straight criminal offences, is that it brings the whole law into disrepute. And the Law is there only to serve the public in whose name it has been passed.

A Thatcher government will therefore be based on the need to gain effective general support on the question of whether as a country we want to be an effective society or not. To some extent it is the same problem which faced the Heath government in 1974. But we have since paid dearly in terms of vast increases in inflation and the failure of the Labour government to meet this problem.

Essentially the failure of the Heath government was a failure in communication. Not only did people not really understand the gravity of the situation but they were prepared to accept that Labour might be able to provide an effective alternative remedy. Now they have seen, in terms of roaring inflation and soaring unemployment, that this was very far from the case. It has become instead a question of mobilising democracy to defend itself, or gaining the open support of public opinion to say what people have been privately saying in their own homes, in the pub and in the bus queue increasingly in recent months.

From this point of view the women's role is obviously going to be of crucial importance. It was women who, to a considerable extent, put the Conservatives in power in 1970. It was women who became increasingly alarmed by the effects of inflation and who turned away from the Tories in 1974. Where are they likely to stand now on the issue of a female Prime Minister to cope with their difficulties?

Margaret Thatcher is far too honest and far too experienced a politician to go consciously after the female vote. To approach women as a separate group within the community who can be swayed by particular policies is to reduce politics to the position illustrated by one of the most famous stories told about Harold Wilson. 'Why,' he is alleged to have said, addressing a meeting in a dockyard constituency, 'do I place such emphasis on the future of the Royal Navy?' 'Because,' shouted back a voice from the audience, 'you're speaking in Chatham.'

What is important is whether Margaret Thatcher is able to put over the issues which affect everybody in ways which other women understand and whether, after she has won an election, she can identify them with the need to succeed on what she regards as the vital issues. Here it is very important that she does speak, for the first time as a major party leader, with feminine logic in a way that women can understand. To a considerable extent, when the predominantly male composition of the Conservative Parliamentary Party elected her as their leader, they changed history in a way which the majority of them did not fully understand at the time.

Other women have been successful Prime Ministers in other countries. In India Mrs Gandhi, and in Sri Lanka (Ceylon) Mrs Bandaranaike were the successors to family traditions in which their names carried considerable emotive support and in areas where educated women had already started to take an increasingly dominant part in politics generally. In Israel, Mrs Meir was generally accepted as everybody's grandmother and was identified, as a result of her marvellously warm and outgoing personality, with the particular problems and aspirations of what is still a small nation.

In Britain, the situation is a much more interesting and unusual one. Margaret Thatcher has come to the top politically not because of who she is and not because of, but in spite of, the fact that she is a woman. She was chosen because, in the face of a good deal of able male competition, she was the best person for the job. Now that that decision has been made, it would be foolish to suggest that a woman Prime Minister is going to be exactly the same as a male one, whatever party she belongs to. The electors of the Sutton Division of Plymouth had an equally free choice when they returned Nancy Astor to Parliament in 1919. But things were never quite the same again.

If Margaret Thatcher becomes the next Prime Minister of Britain, what will this mean from a practical point of view? In the first place, we will have one of the most logical and practical governments that this country has ever had. Secondly, we will get a period of very open government. Women on the whole tend to be much more direct than men. Fundamentally Margaret Thatcher is likely to be much more concerned with practical events than she will be with the build-up of her own image or her political career. Thirdly, it will be an administration that gets down to fundamentals and which is likely to have the ability to make people feel, in a way that they have not felt for some time, that they are part of the process of government.

It will certainly be as broad-based an administration as possible as far as the Conservative Party is concerned. One of the great capacities that Margaret Thatcher has already shown as party leader has been that of healing the wounds which the run-up for the election of a new leader might have caused. Her shadow cabinet is in fact already working extremely well as a team. Her cabinet, hopefully, would also include Edward Heath, possibly in the role of Foreign Secretary. It would be a total waste of talent at a time when the House of Commons is not over-provided with major figures if he were not ready in the long run to serve the party and the country for which he has done so much and to which he has still got so much to give. The historical precedents of A J Balfour and Sir Alec Douglas-Home would totally justify such a decision. The wasted careers of Lloyd George after 1922 or Enoch Powell today are depressing evidence in the other direction. Certainly from her willingness to use major non-political figures in crucial roles during her period at the Department of Education it would appear that Margaret Thatcher will be willing to bring in suitable people from outside Parliament to play a part.

It is interesting to compare the situation so far as Margaret Thatcher is concerned with that of Shirley Williams, her only potential woman rival on the left. Although Shirley Williams's career in the House of Commons has been one of considerable distinction, she has increasingly become identified with the social democrat wing of the Labour Party only and has become aligned with Roy Jenkins, Reg Prentice and Harold Lever as a figure of the moderate right. It is certainly impossible to imagine Shirley Williams being elected as leader by the

Parliamentary Labour Party on the same basis as Margaret Thatcher was elected by the Conservative Parliamentary Party as a whole.

As Prime Minister where would she stand in relation to other world leaders? Her meetings so far with major figures like Giscard d'Estaing, Trudeau and Kissinger have been impressive. Just as she has shown an awareness of the importance of frank speaking on national issues, so she has been ready to speak up openly on international affairs.

In a major speech which she made to the Chelsea Conservative Association on 27th July 1975, she showed a realistic grasp of the facts of international politics in the 1970s. In purely economic terms, she warned, a united Western Europe might be as strong as the Soviet Union. In military terms it has become much weaker.

'The Soviet Union,' she said, 'spends 20 per cent more each year than the United States on military research and development, 25 per cent more on weapons and equipment and 60 per cent more on strategic nuclear forces. The world's most formidable navy, the Russian navy, is relentlessly extending its power, from the Mediterranean to the Indian Ocean. It is now a global force and has more nuclear submarines than the rest of the world's navies put together. It has more surface ships than could possibly be needed to protect the Soviet Union's own coast and merchant shipping.

'Yet this is the moment when the Labour Government has chosen to start pulling the Royal Navy out of the Mediterranean and to ditch the Simonstown Agreement, under which the Navy shared the Simonstown Base with South Africa.'

She went on to point out the actual nature of Soviet power and the brutality inherent in it.

'We in this country allow full and free expression for the point of view of the Soviet Union and its supporters here. But they have ruthlessly trampled on the ideals of the West in every country where it is in their power to do so.

'Czechoslovakia in 1968 showed that the Soviets are prepared not only to destroy liberty but also to crush systematically any brand of Communism which differs from their own.'

There was a feeling, she said, in Europe, as in Asia, that the parties and people of the United States might be falling into a mood of isolationism.

'This has not happened, but the less willing and able we Europeans become to carry our share of the common burden, the less willing the Americans will be to man the defences with us. An isolationist Britain would encourage an isolationist America.'

The Western Governments must, she insisted, stand firm in their dealings with the Russians. The whole history of negotiations with the Soviet Union should teach us that if we did something they wanted without insisting on something in return, the Soviets did not regard it as a kindness to be reciprocated but as a weakness to be exploited.

'We must work for a real relaxation of tension, but in our negotiations with the Eastern bloc we must not accept words or gestures as a substitute for genuine detente.

'No flood of words emanating from a Summit Conference will mean anything unless it is accompanied by some positive action by which the Soviet leaders show their ingrained attitudes are really beginning to change.

'That is why we so strongly support all those European and American spokesmen who have insisted that no serious advance towards a stable peace can be made unless some progress at least is seen in the free movement of people and ideas.

'We must be firm in our desire for a real detente—provided it is real. We must work hard for disarmament provided it is genuine and balanced.

'But let us accept no proposals which would tip the balance of power still further against the West. The power of NATO is already at its lowest safe limit.

'We will be alert not to miss the moment when the Soviets turn to genuine detente, but until that is achieved we must quietly determine to maintain western military strength at a level adequate to deter any aggression.

'It is worth drawing the attention of some of our more gullible disarmers to the fact that if we reduce our conventional forces further, then should hostilities break out there would be no effective middle course between surrender or the early rise of nuclear weapons.

'Serious and solid negotiation is the only way to real detente and lasting peace. In this dangerous world we must never allow the momentum of reconciliation to slacken. While we must work for a world based on peace and trust,' she stressed, 'it would be foolish as well as dangerous to pretend that we have achieved it merely by saying so. Moscow must be challenged to prove that agreement is based on actions as well as words.'

It was a remarkable speech, not the less remarkable because it was her first major pronouncement on foreign affairs since becoming the party leader. She had clearly taken great pains with preparing it since it was to represent her broad view of the subject. She was obviously determined that it should express not only her own deeply felt commitment to the cause of peace but also her belief that peace does not come easily but is only achieved by frank speaking and hard work.

In terms of foreign politics, this represents an important aspect of her philosophy that little or nothing in politics can be achieved the easy way but that we need to work at defending things that we take for granted whether it be the balance of power, our defences or our own liberties. As she also said in her Chelsea speech:

'When the Soviet leaders jail a writer or a priest, or a doctor or a worker, for the crime of speaking freely, it is not only for humanitarian reasons that we should be concerned. For these acts reveal a country that is afraid of truth and liberty; it does not allow its people to enjoy the freedom that we take for granted, and a nation that denies these freedoms to its own people will have few scruples in denying them to others.'

These are sentiments which a good many people in this country feel but which many have become chary of expressing lest they should appear to be too hard-line or too outspoken. It is not the least of Margaret Thatcher's qualities that she does not hesitate, when necessary, to speak her mind and it will be an important aspect of her achievement if she can manage to restore this element of frank speaking to the currency of everyday political debate on an international as well as a national level.

14

When Will She Lead the Country?

British politics, like many other things in Britain, have changed very considerably over the last ten years. If one reads, for instance, Anthony Howard and Richard West's account of the 1964 election, *The Making of the Prime Minister*, they might be writing about a completely different era to the present one. True enough, that particular election, when Harold Wilson fought for the first time as Labour leader and won by a majority of four seats after a lengthy period of Conservative rule since 1951, was to mark the beginning of a significant degree of change. During that campaign *The Economist* even felt able to advocate a Labour victory 'on the nicest balance'. The atmosphere of comparative consensus in the middle ground, at any rate as far as economic and industrial affairs were concerned, that had given rise to the somewhat dubious description 'Butskellism', from an amalgamation of the names of R A Butler and Hugh Gaitskell, still seemed to apply.

From that time on there was to be a marked alteration of temperature in the political scene and a good deal of conscious or unconscious shifting in the position of both the leading parties. During the 1950s and the first part of the 1960s the Conservatives seemed the natural government party. Labour was apparently in constant disarray, torn by a series of internal ideological wars over disarmament, over nationalisation, over the degree of state control that should be applied to the economy, so that a Penguin Special was even published under the title *Must Labour Lose?* Harold Wilson's narrow win in 1964, paving the way for his more effective victory in 1966, opened the possiblity of two developments. Although his second government ended in nearly total disaster, Labour had been able to establish themselves as a persuasive alternative government. And the left wing of the Socialist Party realised that the door was wide open to swing the movement further left than it had been at any time since the war.

The election of 1966 is, in fact, the only one that Harold Wilson has won by a substantial majority. Edward Heath's victory in 1970, after Wilson had thought that he had got his timing right for a quick dash to safety, undoubtedly came as a considerable shock to the Labour leader. For the first few months of the new Parliament he physically gave the impression of a man who has been struck by lightning, and an equal aura of gloom and divisiveness hung around the Parliamentary Labour Part as a whole. It was Wilson's major achievement, for his own party, that in this difficult period he managed to hold them together in an effective form of party unity. The price that he paid for this was to become increasingly dependent on the good will of the left wing. When Roy Jenkins resigned as Harold Wilson's deputy over the issue of European entry, the balance in effect tipped in favour of the Tribune Group and, whatever the respective numbers at any time within the Parliamentary Labour Party itself, the impetus lay with the Marxist rather than the Social Democrat wing within the party.

There was also an almost imperceptible swing towards the left in the composition of Labour Members of Parliament during the period after 1970. The two elections of 1974 brought in a number of new members of far left-wing views, while in other individual constituency parties the left began to capture power and get rid of members of whom they disapproved on ideological grounds like Dick Taverne and Eddie Griffiths.

What was happening in the House of Commons was also to a considerable extent being mirrored by what was happening in the trade union movement. Not only did Jack Jones, Hugh Scanlon and Arthur Scargill represent a new degree of ideological militancy within the unions, but they had established by the apparent ease of their victories over Edward Heath in 1972 and 1974 the implicit suggestion that trade union militancy must apparently succeed whatever the realities of the issue.

As a result of this a serious difficulty became inherent for any potential Conservative Prime Minister—the feeling that a Conservative Government must start under the potential threat that in the event of any possible confrontation with the unions they were bound to have the effective power to get what they wanted. Although both the elections in 1974 showed that there was certainly no majority in favour of the militants they seemed to be in the unanswerable position of having the whip hand.

A fundamental question therefore seemed to be posed over the future of the

Tory Party itself. Given a situation of the 1974 confrontation type, could a Conservative Government hold out policies, even if these were supported by a majority of the electorate, if they were opposed by a section of the TUC involved in key industries? In these circumstances could a Conservative Government pursue distinctive policies however much they felt these to be right and in the national interest if they ran contrary to the stated objects of the more militant union leaders and therefore might lead to the possibility of confrontation? Had we now reached a stage where the real power in the country must always lie in the hands of those figures in the unions who had the power to sanction strike action, either as a threat or as a fact, as a method of bringing the highly complex and interdependent system of industry in this country to a standstill and therefore any government to its knees?

The issue involved is very much the one which defeated the Heath Government in February 1974 and which produced the events that were described in the first chapter of this book. As a straight question of 'Who governs the country?' it led them into an indeterminate situation which seemed to leave the scales weighted in favour of any possible militant action. If this was so and if it portended a continuing situation at least for the forseeable future, had a future Conservative Government any real role to play except as a temporary check on an inevitable march towards a full-scale Socialist state in this country? Would any Labour Government be more than a Parliamentary cypher to put into legislative effect the views of whoever controlled the larger unions? Did this mean that power had passed from Parliament for ever?

The answers to these questions are clearly going to determine what will happen to this country and in what sort of society we are going to live for a good many years to come. To some extent they are obviously likely to be influenced by developments which take place over the next few years. They are also liable to depend, however, to a very considerable degree on how people as a whole react to the forthcoming political scene.

From this aspect the position of Margaret Thatcher is likely to be of crucial importance. There is no doubt that the great majority of people in this country do not want, any more than the people of Portugal do, a full-blooded Socialist state. There is, equally, little doubt that public opinion as a whole is extremely uncertain what can or should be done to meet the nations' difficulties and dangers, particularly the overweening menace of inflation. The failure of Labour's first attempt to establish effective control over the explosion of wage inflation by means of the social contract has left Harold Wilson casting around for an alternative that might prove more effective in cutting down the rate of increase in domestic inflation. Experience has so far shown not only how extremely vulnerable any programme that the Labour Government has proposed must be but that it is entirely dependent, as it stands at present, on the membership of individual unions. As David Wood, the political correspondent of *The Times* has put it, 'As a policy, it may be variously seen as the second phase of Mr Wilson's social contract, made inevitable by the failure of the first phase, or as phase four of the Heath counter-inflationary policy, which brought down the Conservative Government on February 28th, 1974. Neither view offers much encouragement.'

There is certainly some considerable ground for saying that people in Britain have become, particularly during the summer of 1975, increasingly aware of the threat that inflation is creating for them, not only in terms of their own standard of living but in terms also of unemployment figures, of the maintenance of essential government and local government services and of being able to keep either the private sector or the nationalised industries solvent.

This has not stopped, so far, the unprecedented wage demands that have been put forward in a number of vital industries. Many people have been inclined to take the view that, so long as workers in these particular industries are able to protect their own purchasing power by insisting on increased pay packets, then irrespective of the position of the rest of the community, they will be ready to continue with these demands because they will not themselves be directly affected by inflationary pressure. To quote Harold Wilson's phrase, one man's pay rise is another man's price rise. The viability of these increases can be maintained in the short run, in spite of the unreality of such a policy and the effect which it has on the overall level of employment, by borrowing funds from overseas to maintain either the nationalised industries or unprofitable enterprises at their present level for as long as possible. The reality of such a programme as was being operated by Anthony Wedgwood Benn during his period at the Department of Industry is obviously dubious and short-term in the extreme, short of changing the whole system into a pattern of state-subsidised workers' cooperatives or into a siege economy.

Harold Wilson, when interviewed by *Time* magazine in July 1975, took a view of his second round of proposals to establish pay limits which remained buoyant but carried very little effective assurance as to the viability of his methods. In answer to Herman Nickel, chief of *Time*'s London bureau, he said, 'It will be a difficult winter and the real test comes if any individual group were to press (for more than the pay limit). This would have to be a test case but the government are determined to stand absolutely firm.' In defining what sort of action he had in mind, he added: 'We are backing the pay limit with some legislation, not designed to send people to jail, but for example to tighten up the amount of money available to finance excess settlements. What we propose is to reserve powers against maverick or rogue employers, not against workers, but we shall go to great lenghts to avoid having to invoke them. The Trades Union Congress accepted these powers with great reluctance.'

It is significant that at this point in events he still saw any sanctions to achieve a limit to wage inflation as being against maverick or rogue *employers*. When it came to the unions, he said, 'They have no veto but what any government requires is consent. And the problem of getting consent from the unions is satisfying them that they have been fairly treated. What I've always tried to do is not just to get to know trade union leaders but to get to know the people in the districts.'

What exactly this pronouncement means in the face of further potential militant action is hard precisely to say. It is clear that if it came to taking effective powers to enforce a statutory incomes policy Wilson would not only precipitate resignations from the left-wing members of his own cabinet, like Michael Foot, but would face, despite all his expertise, the risk of eventually splitting the Labour Party once and for all on this issue. Left-wing trades unionists like Arthur Scargill have already gone on record as saying that they want Anthony Wedgwood Benn as an alternative leader of the Socialist Party. Once this occurred, if it did, then the split must obviously become complete. In the meantime, left-inclined constituency parties have been inundating the Labour Conference with demands for a further extension of nationalisation in any event, including powers to take insurance, the banks, building societies and other financial organisations that form the basis of a free market economy into public control.

If the Labour Party did split into totally conflicting wings then it would obviously find itself very much in the position that the Liberal Party found itself in after its effective self-dismemberment of 1922. It is hard in any event to see that the left, having tasted the heady wine of Anthony Wedgwood Benn, would accept less than a tacit agreement by the rest of the party to accept a continually escalating move towards further left-wing policies.

What will the next Conservative Government do to meet this situation? In the first place, Margaret Thatcher has accepted, with some vigour, the premise that at this point in the history of this country nothing could be worse than the Conservative Party merely coming to office by default, because Labour was no longer able to cope with Britain's problems, and the swing of the pendulum or, for example, a Parliamentary defeat simply producing an alternative administration. This is effectively what happened to Labour in 1974, when they were elected in reliance on the euphemism of the social contract and had got no effective policies to meet the underlying problems.

When Harold Wilson spoke of 'consent' in his *Time* interview he was putting the facts of the position at a dangerously low level. What must be needed at this point is far more than merely obtaining consent but an actual and effective involvement of the majority of the population in the struggle to succeed. As has already been seen, Margaret Thatcher is a passionate protagonist of the free economy. She believes this because not only does she hold that only by the effective working of a free economy can Britain succeed but it is only by this means that the majority of people there can really achieve a fulfilling existence.

She is fully convinced of the need to mobilise public opinion to support this. She is very well aware that it is going to be no use asking the public as a whole to commit themselves unless three pre-conditions are achieved. There is a need to recognise that it is the root causes of inflation that need to be checked and not merely its symptoms. There is the need to face the fact that the majority of people are not going to accept either the justice or the necessity of a counter-inflationary policy unless it is accompanied by public expenditure cuts. And there is the need to understand that what is required is a real restoration of confidence.

Margaret Thatcher is very well aware of the importance, in this regard, of the middle ground. She understands and can identify with the vast number of people who have felt continually undermined by the immense increase in the cost of living. She is also well aware of the enormous feeling of frustration in that many people feel that so many of our troubles are self-induced and that we have still got the skills and abilities and capacities required if only these could be harnessed to a going concern. Just as people want to feel that they are part and parcel of a thriving firm, so they have a deeply rooted desire to belong to a successful country.

Toryism, in her view, must speak with a distinctive voice. Although the days are long past when it is possible for even the most partisan observer to identify the Tories as a 'bosses' party and the Socialists as a 'workers' party there is a distinction which is vital between the two and that is between belief in individual enterprise and state control. Far too much in recent years the Conservatives have been seen as being a grey party, far too little have they caught the imagination of the aspirations of people who have looked for an alternative creed to Socialism. Far too often the situation has been allowed to go by default. Marxism may be a minority viewpoint in this country, but it is at any rate one which is held with passion by its supporters. If the majority of people believe in free enterprise and opportunity, then they must be galvanised to commit themselves to their beliefs with equal enthusiasm. As Margaret Thatcher said in her speech on her election as leader of the Conservative Party, the price of failure would be incalculable.

There have been Conservatives, just as there have been members of the press, who have been inclined to complain during the summer of 1975 that, having come in on a moment of highly political impetus in February, Margaret Thatcher has been inclined to settle for too low a profile in the House of Commons. There has been talk of a continuing split in the Tory ranks and suggestions that the Conservative decision to abstain from voting against Harold Wilson's second stage package was an attempt to paper over such cracks. Political journalists were quick to seize on Edward Heath's speech from the backbenches in this debate as a deliberate attempt to upstage the new leader. On 28th July, for instance, the *Evening Standard* Londoner's Diary carried a paragraph about a talk on sailing which Edward Heath had given on the radio which seemed to suggest that the former leader was merely waiting his turn in the wings.

'Thatcher-custodians and between-the-line readers,' it ran, 'can make what they will of Mr Heath's remark, "I prefer to skipper. I never do crew for other people." Was it just coincidence that he pushed the *double entendre* further when asked about the difficulty of ocean racing. "You may appear to be going in exactly the wrong direction, and then later you emerge in front," said Mr Heath. "Time will tell."' There has been a good deal of similar press speculation of the same sort.

One of the problems of our present unsettled political period is that we are too inclined to look for instant remedies. The sort of criticism that has been levelled against Margaret Thatcher seems a misunderstanding both of the situation and of what she is trying to do. Of all people, her track record shows that she would be the least likely to go for an easy answer. What she has done in the recent months since her election has been to establish her base both in Parliament and the country, to take careful stock of the position and to begin the major task of putting the real issues before people in the country.

As John Marling said of her, she is certainly not someone to jump in in the House and speak for the sake of speaking. During her first years as a backbencher in Parliament she spoke comparatively rarely, but when she did people listened to her. Now she is speaking regularly in different parts of Britain and doing so with immense impact.

The electors are sick and tired of factious politics. What is involved now is too important for the mere enjoyment of debating points. If the Conservatives had voted with the government on the July anti-inflation provisions they would have been rubber-stamping an insufficiently prepared and explained programme that gave no real explanation of how Harold Wilson intended to meet the continuing crisis. If they had gone into the lobby with the Tribune Group to oppose the provisions, they would have given the appearance of trying to shut the door to the present elected government's final attempt to get to grips with the problems.

It would be a rash individual, particularly a politician, who tried to prophesy too exactly what is going to happen over the next few months. A week in politics is still a very long time. Just as Harold Wilson based his short-term strategy on the social contract and his long-term hopes on North Sea oil, so he now seems to be founding his continuing expectations on the prospect of a general reflation in other Western economies that might ease the pressures on inflation-hit Britain.

Frighteningly, for the country, the situation seems to be not much different from the later years of his earlier period of government in the late 1960s. Other governments were then looking keenly at the British economy to see whether we had any intention of finding an effective way out of our industrial difficulties. When the then Labour Government under Wilson back-pedalled on its policies there was a considerable increase in international scepticism at the unviability of Britain's position.

Britain is now once more in an alarmingly high debtor–creditor ratio with overseas nations, particularly with the Middle East. The position of our economy is such that it only needs a comparatively small adverse gust to blow us violently off course, such as, for instance, a possible substantial increase in the price charged for oil by the consortium of oil-producing nations. Against this background it is absolutely vital that we should be seen to be doing everything within our power to set our own house in order.

Unfortunately, the Labour Party's refusal to accept wage demands as being a fundamental aspect of inflation in this country does not bode particularly well for the economic future. As Harold Wilson admitted it is a question not just of agreeing a form of wording with the TUC but of persuading the members of the individual unions where their actual interests lie. An added difficulty both for Wilson and for the country lies in the number of activists in certain unions who would be only too ready to let the whole system collapse in order to replace it by an entirely different state.

One way and another, the Labour Government's chances of surviving for anything like its full term of office seem increasingly slender. Like Harold Wilson in 1964, it could be that Margaret Thatcher may have only a comparatively short period of preparation as leader of the Opposition before she is called on to fight an election.

She herself is obviously ready and prepared for such an eventuality. She is also very well aware of the importance of this election when it comes. Politicians frequently speak of each coming election as being the most important one there has been for years. In the present case there is absolutely no doubt that this is true.

In preparing for the election, whenever it does come, she has taken into account not only the significance of the issues involved, but of the way in which her case is going to be presented. What sort of form it will take is by no means clear, whether it will be a question of the Conservative Party fighting the two distinct sections of the Labour Party as separate units or whether Harold Wilson or whoever else leads the Socialists will be able to retain a façade of party unity at the price of still further concessions to the left. But in either case the central issue will remain the same.

In any general election the position of a party leader, though of fundamental importance, is always a difficult one to assess. The personalities of the two leaders may be of great effect but they are only relevant insofar as they are the means of effectively projecting what each of them stands for.

The Conservative Party is lucky in Margaret Thatcher. They chose her by the most democratic method of election of any of their leaders. In choosing a woman they showed a great deal of confidence in her. In many ways she stands in a position which is unique in the country's history. In a time of change she is a very modern figure but she stands unhesitatingly for the traditional values on which this country has been based. She is fully conscious of the need for Britain to play her full part in Europe and in the world at large. She is also fully determined that the role we should play should be based on our own endeavours and on the place that she believes we can still earn for ourselves in the world by standing on our own feet.

No one could doubt her courage, her determination and her compassion. She has got both the intelligence and the will to mobilise a united Britain into overcoming our economic difficulties and the overwhelming risk to our society that these represent. The measure of her success will be whether she can unify all sections of that society into supporting a revival in this country which will produce a future for Britain which is open to balanced and just opportunity.

That it can be done is proved by the success which has come to France since 1958. In the 1950s France stood in an even lower position, economically, politically and in terms of morale than Britain does today. Today she is still the beneficiary of a remarkable revival. While one would hesitate to draw a comparison between the characters of Charles de Gaulle and Margaret Thatcher, there is certainly one thing which is common to both of them and that is a passionate belief in the future of their own country.

As Margaret Thatcher herself has said, it can all be done. There is such a thing as a faith which can move mountains—but it requires a bit of planning and a bit of muscle as well.

Index

Wood, David 37, 141
Woollcott, Councillor 47, 50
Woollcott, Mrs 47, 48, 49
Woolsack, The 20
Woolton, The Rt Hon Lord 97
World At One, The 26
World Cup, The 65
Worth, Squadron-Leader G. A. 37

Yorkshire 31
Young Conservatives Annual Conference 31
Young Conservatives Association 31
Young Conservatives Association, Colchester 45
Young-Jamieson, Miss 36

Y

Yeovil 23

Z

Zurich 96